Views From the Other Side of the Altar

By Father Justin Lopina

Printed in the United States of America

ISBN 978-0-692-99097-1

First Printing, 2018

Cover Design and Illustrations by Jennifer Robin Meyer

Dedicated to my grandmother, Marian Lopina.

Born to eternity on the Feast Day of Saint Justin: June 1st, 2017.

Without her influence and faith, this book would not have been possible.

Foreword

I wrote a humor-laced foreword, and rewrote it after I realized I was introducing the Padre J-Dawg's humor (which, if you're reading this aloud, might make you the first to ever call him that: the only joke I felt inclined to keep), and not an introduction to the Padre and his tales.

Let me introduce Father Justin Lopina. I've known him most of my life. In 1993, our school class made Christmas tree ornaments: little books with pieces of students' writing in them. Most kids wrote about presents, Santa, or wintry weather.

Like a handful, Justin's wrote about family:

> My most remembered Christmas was 1989. My two cousins came
> to spend the night, and the basement was finished. We played with
> them for about an hour. Then we went into our basement and
> played a game where two people are trying to steal, and two cops
> are making sure they are not. Then they switch. The winner is
> whoever has the most stolen things. My team won. We played
> three more games until lunch. My brother an I sat at the counter,
> while my sister and two cousins sat at the table. We were served,
> and everybody ate quickly. We went to my dad to see if the
> Nintendo was set. The second we saw him we knew it was set.
> How? He was playing it. He let my brother and younger cousin,
> Kimberly, play after he lost. Soon dinner came. Mom was praying
> and grandma put the food on the table. While dad was serving me, I

leaned back. The dog pulled on my chair, and I fell back. I hit my
head, but there was no blood. I have never grown hair there, but it's
covered. We went to bed in my room since I have bunk beds and
places on the floor for three sleeping bags. We told ghost stories
and went to sleep one...by...one. Guess who stayed up the longest?

I happened upon this ornament that I did not myself remember, and I realized a level of
consistency with the Padre's more recent writings. Family, and people are the core of the story.
A sense of place: a sense of place in his surroundings grounds it. Sure, there were some missing
paragraph breaks. The only material present is a prop for sharing, an experience to be shared by
all. There's a lesson from a father about letting the little ones, the lesser ones, go first. A tad bit
of drama, and some entertaining emphasis. Maybe it's the curse of having studied English, but I
see consistency from the Padre's writing of 24 years ago to today's. I also see consistency in his
values and character.

Those values are why I was honored when Justin asked me to write one of his reference
letters for seminary. My only reservation, and I expressed this, was that Justin would have made
a great (biological) father. Mayhap my protestant understanding of Catholic dogma left me a
hair short of true insight as to the meaning of the title "Father". He is now one of a small handful
of people I see as excellent fathers in my life. He is also someone I feel comfortable talking
about religious and spiritual concerns with, and not just my curiosity about the workings of the
Catholic Church, which to this protestant, seems slightly confusing at times.

We have similar sense of humor, and there's a fair bit of it in the Father's writings. It
might be one factor that makes him appeal to people outside his parishioners, bringing a strong
aura of humanity that disarms those often made defensive by a representative of organized

religion. He ministers to many who seem inclined to stand as far from The Church as they can, spreading care instead of condemnation.

During our college years and his subsequent Peace Corps years, Justin and I communicated little. Not of any emotional distance, but geographical circumstance. On his one break from Peace Corps, he surprised me at my house one morning as I was heading to bed following a 3rd shift. I was happy to forego sleep that day. It's people that are important to him, as well as to me.

It has been a joy to read, and offer suggestions, on the Padre's first book. I do not claim to be the perfect editor, and I do not claim we had the perfect process, but it's our first go. I hope you find some insight into a priest of this generation, one who is a voice that resonates to those in the flock, but also somehow clearly to those sheep wandering the hillsides, ears overgrown with wool, usually hearing only muffled sounds. His voice sounds more clearly than many to those outside, who have looked with doubt on the Catholic Church, and even Christianity. I say so with certainty, as his voice speaks clearly to me. These are tales of a person of good deeds, compassion, learning, and growth. They also have confusion, mistakes, disappointment, joy, redemption and hope.

I hope Father Justin's voice also speaks to you, kind reader. May you find peace and insight, and human compassion in the pages that follow.

– Robert C. Kellner, Jan 9th, 2018

Acknowledgements

Very few achievements in life can be considered a fully individual victory. With staggering frequency, that sense of victory and success belongs to a group of people working toward a common goal together. This book is proof enough of that: a self-published book describing a series of personal reflections. With certainty that I could not do it alone, I thank the people most directly involved in this book's completion:

First and foremost, my unending thanks goes to Robert Kellner for his role as editor. The sheer difference of quality between the first and final drafts is staggering and humbling. For all intends and purposes, if a portion of the book especially strikes you, it is either due to Rob's direct contribution or indirect encouragement.

In that same spirit of teamwork, thanks go to Robin Meyer for her illustrations. When we graduated from Beloit College in 2004, I always knew that my friend Robin would be my first choice for any artwork I'd require in life.

Finally, I offer my thanks to Lex Cashore, as a representative of all the people who offered their encouragement to my efforts. Early in the writing process, Lex ready the first draft of my chapter on superstition, and immediately begged for more. I've heard it said that the Devil is, among other things, The Accuser. He's the voice in your head that tells you that you suck and that you should quit whatever it is you're doing. When he dropped in to convince me that this whole thing was pointless, it was ultimately Lex's voice that beat it back down. So fully aware of the irony, thank you, Lex, for your faith in me. It did not go to waste.

Contents

Chapter One: People Are Made of Glass

One flesh, one bone

One true religion

One voice, one hope

One real decision

Gimmie one vision

–One Vision, by Queen

To write the statement "people are made of glass" is a tricky thing, because the thought is a product of several origins that one day came together by way of life experience, non-fiction regarding life experience, and non-fiction regarding fairy tales. I will also explain this viewpoint while resisting the temptation to reference *The Glass Menagerie*. That would be a bit too obvious. Perhaps the fairy tales should indeed be the first place to explore.

The fairy tales in question are primarily "Cinderella" and "Sleeping Beauty". However, there is an element of glass in several other minor fairy tales - although mirrors mainly represent something different from their non-reflective cousins. GK Chesterton, in his defense of the Christian religion *Orthodoxy*, explains that in fairy tales, glass represents human happiness (Orthodoxy, ch 2, loc 755). It is a fragile and breakable thing, and one quick impact will destroy it entirely. Glass can be destroyed intentionally as well as accidently - a wayward sway of an arm or a momentary loss of one's grip will cause a wine glass to shatter on the floor. Even a harmless kitten has the means to break a glass that is left unattended. However, Chesterton also states "that to be breakable is not the same as to be perishable" (ibid, loc 760). Glass may be broken in a matter of seconds, but if cared for properly, a glass object can endure for a thousand years or more. Every so often, I think of this lesson as watch someone texting on their phone with an utterly destroyed screen. The image of fractured and splintered happiness is an easy one to recollect in such moments. Of course, while one's technology can be fractured and broken for all to see, a *person's* brokenness is far harder to recognize. Could that person be just as cracked as their screen?

Moving on to the non-fiction regarding life experience, I received some excellent advice from a Rabbi in the summer of 2012. I was attending a Christian/Jewish ecumenical conference in Connecticut one year before my deaconate ordination and about one month before a three-month hospital chaplain program. At this conference mainly comprised of people seeking out a vocation in ministry (be it Jewish, Catholic, or Protestant), one of the major themes of our talks and discussions was the commonality between the two faiths. Our first speaker, Irving Greenberg, spoke briefly about his book *For the Sake of Heaven and Earth: The New Encounter between Judaism and Christianity*, and his overall experience as a Jewish religious leader.

One piece of practical advice hit me, and it was short and sweet enough to remember verbatim. "When you preach, or otherwise speak to your congregation, stretch them by 10%." Frankly, that made all the sense in the world to me. So often, as teachers in some way, we try to snap people from side of a vast gulf to the other. We hope that with a great argument, people will see reason and change their ways. Of course, life is not so simple. People cannot change by 100% all at once. If they try, they break. However, people can change by 10%. With one clear step to begin, people can be stretched; they bend without breaking, and with time they might very well reach the 20% mark without any additional guidance or encouragement. Sometimes, the beginning of the journey is enjoyable enough to warrant the journey's continuation.

Those two little lessons were floating around my head by the time priesthood rolled around I actually began speaking to people as a spiritual leader with an authoritative voice. After all, when I speak at Sunday Mass, people pay attention... whether they agree with what I say or not. Every so often, the message of my homily is a bit over a 10% stretch, and the goal I was attempting to achieve goes up in smoke in an instant. That is always something of a shame, and I always leave with the suspicion that a more gentle and gradual stretch would have been the solution for that person from the start. Of course, "stretch people by 10%" is a subjective command: the 10% in question is partially dependent upon the individual recipient. After all, everyone may not start a race in the same place. For the sake of illustrating this point in particular, I can think of four Sunday homilies where at least one person was not stretched by 10%. From there, we will return to the concept of shattering people like glass.

The first homily that comes to mind was one I titled "Physical, Emotional, and Spiritual Damage", given while I was still a deacon and one year away from priesthood. This was one of the more esoteric of my homilies, because I chose to express my central idea through the use of a tabletop RPG (role-playing game) rulebook. The game in question was a lovely little product called *Deleria: Fairy Tales for a New Millennium*. I cared about this book so much, I brought my large hardcover copy to Africa during my Peace Corps service. Peace Corps tells its new recruits, in no uncertain terms, that books are one of the largest wastes of space when packing for your two-year service. There are plenty of books waiting for you in your country of service, and you need the space for American products that you cannot purchase overseas. I didn't follow that rule terribly well, with *Deleria* being the most obvious piece of evidence.

Anyway, one page of the book detailed the way characters took damage in combat or other forms of conflict. You see, the bulk of role-playing games' rules essentially boil down to conflict, or whether or not a character's action succeeds. Games for beginners keep it simple: you have 100 points of "life", and when you lose them all, you're dead. Other games strive for accuracy and realism - they include rules for blood loss, broken bones, and fatigue. It all depends upon the system and its target demographic. *Deleria*, essentially a rule book for new age fairy tales, went out of its way to explain the difference between physical, mental, and spiritual damage. After all, in fairy tales, not all enemies are simple warriors with swords and armor; they are schoolyard bullies, abusive coworkers, demons, or dangerous desires made manifest. Therefore, bodily damage is not the only sort of danger a person ought to be prepared to defend against. I happened to dearly appreciate the distinction, and I hoped to impart the lesson to my general congregation in spite of their ignorance of the RPG.

I wrote and gave this homily on the appropriate Sunday, and with ties to Scripture, I illustrated the difference between visible pain on one's body versus the emotional/spiritual pain that no one else sees unless we cry out for help. I still believe that the homily was well-written and concise. Whatever failure I may have experienced, I don't think it was poor writing or unclear public speaking. Rather, I believe that it was too detached and/or unrelatable for people to understand within an eight-minute presentation. My father respectfully told me that the homily was "ok", but far from my best. My pastor gave it a "C+", which was the lowest grade he ever gave me, and no one approached me after Mass to tell me that the homily moved them or taught them something special. Of course, that is not a big deal, and hardly cause to consider it a total failure. It simply means that it didn't strike anyone to the core, or stretch anyone by 10%.

One parishioner, with great admiration for me, asked where that information came from. I explained it to her, and even gave her a few photocopies of the relevant pages of the book. A week later, she updated me and said that it was all just too much for her to take in. She spent the rest of her time raving about the homily I gave a month earlier. In short, I tried to stretch people more than 10%. As I have been playing RPGs since I was 13 years old, I forgot how alien those books can be to someone who's never encountered one before. I still believe in the message... I just need to find a way to state it in more ordinary terms when speaking to non-gamers.

The second homily in question was also during my deaconate year, which is like a year of on-the-job training before ordination to the priesthood. For my year as a deacon, I couldn't say Mass or hear confessions, but I was permitted to teach, visit in the hospital, have occasional weddings or funerals, and preach at a Mass in place of the priest. My failure to stretch people by 10% was absurdly obvious to me after the fact, because it happened to be the one Sunday of my entire deaconal year when a priest from the seminary came to my parish to hear my preaching and ask the general congregation about my overall ability in the pulpit and effect on their lives. I knew that he would be coming on this particular weekend, so I intentionally prepared a funny homily - a homily where I made myself the object of ridicule. To that extent, I succeeded. I told a story about how I was totally entranced by a cute saleswoman at the mall while Christmas shopping. She was so effective, she sold me three do-it-yourself nail buffing kits (one for my mom, one for my sister, and one for myself). I followed the story up with the point that the saleswoman needed to be clever to sell me a product I had a genuine use of, because I wouldn't have recognized its value by any other means. Jesus was clever; Jesus told his disciples to be clever; Jesus tells us all to be clever; that saleswoman was clever. I believed that the connection between my theological point and my story was solid and clear. As my seminary professor and I discovered after Mass, the connection was not as solid as I had hoped. The good news was that practically everyone was highly entertained, and because I was making fun of myself, people felt free to laugh without restraint.

The ultimate problem was that I failed to stretch people by any amount at all - let alone 10%. My homily was, ironically, too funny: it didn't challenge anyone to think more deeply about Jesus-style cleverness. The seminary priest stopped people after Mass and asked them "so what was Deacon Justin's homily about?" All across the board, people answered in a similar fashion:

"Oh! It was about how Deacon Justin got tricked into buying too many things at the mall!"

"Deacon Justin got his nails buffed by a cute girl, but he was too embarrassed to tell anyone about it until now!"

"Deacon Justin cares for his nails, even to this day."

6

After everyone's response, I desperately asked "what else was the homily about?" Of the two dozen people-or-so people that were interviewed, no one was able to connect my story to the Gospel story, and no one mentioned my appeal to Christ's general call to cleverness.

In the end, the story was simply too entertaining. People listened to me, laughed with me and at me, and left for home without any real change to their spiritual lives. I didn't teach them anything, I didn't push them to new heights of moral excellence, and I didn't challenge them to see the world a little bit differently. I simply told a funny story, and I got a few laughs as a result. In order to really help people grow, we not only need to provide the way and we need to illuminate the ultimate destination. That Sunday, my true failure was exactly that illumination of destination. My congregation understood my story... they just didn't understand where it was meant to lead them.

The next homily that comes to mind was well received and most people appreciated the amount of humor. In fact, the failure to stretch people by 10% was only a bit of a failure - only a few people took issue with my message, and they were only bothered by a single sentence. The homily was primarily about wisdom, and the perpetual need for us all to grow in wisdom. To make this point, I told one of my favorite "men versus women" stories. One of our traditions in high school was a summer bonfire, with all my friends in one place. It was a great time, and I dearly remember that evening to this day. Well, knowing that there would be a large fire available, a male friend of mine brought some flour to the party. You see, a bit of flour tossed onto open flame will puff up into a small fireball. Although I don't recommend this to any of my readers, it was harmless enough... for a while. Later into the evening, after the little flour fireball trick got old, a "brilliant" idea occurred to me.

"Hey guys! You know what we should do? We should all grab two fists full of flour each, and throw it on the fire at the same time! It'll be so cool!" All the guys expressed their enthusiasm for what was surely the best idea of the evening... and all the girls took two or three steps away from the fire.

The story ended with a wall of fire, a 16-year-old Justin flailing in fear, and the guy next to me losing about an inch of his beard and a fair portion of his arm hair. After the church-goers' giggles died down a bit, I made my point. Could the guys have shown greater wisdom? Absolutely. That seems like a difficult point to contest. We certainly could have considered what we were about to do: five seconds of brain activity would have spared us the horrible ending that was ours by right. However, I then asked the congregation whether or not the girls could have shown greater wisdom. To that question, I answered "yes". Indeed, the girls could have been wiser at that moment. Sure, they saved themselves, but they failed to warn us of our folly! They merely stepped back and left us to our own adolescent foolishness.

I thought my point was pretty solid, but a parishioner I knew well caught me after Mass. She proceeded to explain to me that the girls did not have a failure of wisdom. Rather, the girls knew that the guys would never have taken their advice and were wise to stay out of it entirely. To that feedback, I laughed and agreed that we probably would not have listened to reason. I promised to include an extra line, in the event that I felt the desire to repeat the homily in three years (when the readings repeated at Mass). Did I stretch people by 10% that day? Absolutely. I had a good message that day that hopefully 99% of the people enjoyed. However, the parishioner who spoke to me after Mass reminded me that people are, in fact, made of glass. It doesn't take much to shatter them, or rattle their sense of peace, and one simple statement can hit them at just the right angle to ruin their day. All of us try to avoid such a thing, but after a few months of priesthood - where I speak to many people in a short time - I now have a greater appreciation for exactly how fragile people can be. If I rattle people because of one less-than-ideal sentence while preaching, how often do we rattle one another around the dinner table at Thanksgiving? Or in a classroom? Or, dare I suggest it, over the internet? People are more fragile than we often expect. So be gentle.

For my final homiletic example, I can't help but draw attention to a near-perfect ideal that absolutely met the needs of the congregation as a whole. However, one person and one person alone remained upset with me, and left the church with his basic spiritual needs unmet. The homily I'm referring to was one I gave two weeks after the Supreme Court ruled in favor of marriage equality - which Catholic teaching is by-and-large against. My pastor and I agreed that it was a piece of public news that was significant enough to merit a response from us on a Sunday, although we almost never refer to current events or news trends in general. We also agreed to stick to a relatively similar message of care, forgiveness, inclusiveness, and non-judgment. The homily I chose to give depended upon the fact that all people (Catholics and non-Catholics alike) were deeply divided on the issue, which meant that I did not want to agree with a portion of the church at the expense of everyone else. Once that fact was clear in my mind, the rest of the words came easily. I stated clearly that people were divided and that I could not please everyone by agreeing with a particular opinion. I explained that I respected all four major opinions on the matter, and I said it in such a way that I didn't contradict church teaching. The four major opinions, as I understand them, are:

1. The Church is right and everyone else is misled. One man, one woman, period.

2. It's time to change and catch up with the rest of the world. Compassion and equality are what Jesus cares about, period.

3. Just leave me out of it.

4. You're not a politician, you're a priest. Stick to the Bible and leave the current events to others, please.

My pastor described my message as "poetic," and said that I had certainly taken the high road. After I gave it, I lost track of the people who thanked me for bravely tackling a tough issue with so much compassion and wisdom. A couple people at the early Mass actually cried at one point, which is not a typical reaction! Finally, a non-Catholic friend from college watched the clip on YouTube - I wasn't even know that she was aware of them. Well, she reposted the video to her friends and urged them to watch it. Her overall advertisement was "you need to watch this video - he says the opposite of what you'd expect a Catholic priest to say," which was a compliment. She credited me for providing a message that applied to Catholics and non-Catholics alike, and she was thankful for the fact that I was true to my values and yet respectful to the people who don't share those values. I considered that endorsement a huge win across the board!

All that goodness, nevertheless, brings us to the one guy not stretched by 10%. There's a pretty good chance you know the sort of guy I'm referring to. He was an older gentleman, always with a sour look on his face, who mainly speaks to complain. This was a parishioner that would use the old Catholic Guilt Trick to get me to attend men's group meetings, and he once stopped me at the grocery store in town when we happened to run into each other. He lectured me for a while, and described a priest in Florida that had his respect: if I could only be like that other priest, then surely my church's woes would be over in a heartbeat. For the most part, I smile and hear him out, and try not to let him bend me out of shape. Well, on this particular Sunday after my last Mass, beaming with compliments and my general post-Mass glow, he stopped me after I finished saying my goodbyes and have-a-good-days. He just looked me in the eyes and asked me point blank: "You never actually said it, you know. What do you think about the Supreme Court decision? Is it bad or not?"

He was clearly trying to get me to condemn same-sex marriage, as well as the Supreme Court and the rest of the world in general. I refused to take the bait, and said something diplomatic and fatherly. Given the limited time I had to respond, I did alright, but he didn't buy it. He grumbled something under his breath and shuffled off to his car. I saw him a couple of weeks later, and he seemed to be back to his old "mostly grumpy" self. So I concluded little if any actual damage was done that day by my refusal to give him what he wanted.

Of course, his answer is clearly available in Church teaching. The website for the United States Conference of Catholic Bishops (http://www.usccb.org/issues-and-action/marriage-and-family/marriage/promotion-and-defense-of-marriage/questions-and-answers-about-marriage-and-same-sex-unions.cfm) states the matter quite clearly:

> 6. Does denying marriage to homosexual persons demonstrate unjust discrimination and a lack of respect for them as persons?
>
> It is not unjust to deny legal status to same-sex unions because marriage and same-sex unions are essentially different realities. In fact, justice requires society to do so. To uphold God's intent for marriage, in which sexual relations have their proper and exclusive place, is not to offend the dignity of homosexual persons. Christians must give witness to the whole moral truth and oppose as immoral both homosexual acts and unjust discrimination against homosexual persons. The *Catechism of the Catholic Church* urges that homosexual persons "be accepted with respect, compassion, and sensitivity" (no. 2358). It also encourages chaste friendships. "Chastity is expressed notably in *friendship with one's neighbor*. Whether it develops between persons of the same or opposite sex, friendship represents a great good for all" (no. 2347).

In other words, the Catholic Church says in black and white text that while we are certainly called to offer respect and care to all people (no matter their sexuality), same-sex

11

unions are an entirely different nature than marriage. Hence, the Church does not support the decision of the United States Supreme Court.

Was my parishioner stretched by 10% that day? Probably not; I had the impression that he wanted the black & white argument from the very beginning. My attempted message was not to ignore Catholic teaching; it was simply an urging for us all to maintain a unity of faith, in spite of widely differing opinions. Maybe my message of "cool it and don't tear each other's throats out" got through to him after-the-fact, but I doubt it. From my earlier dealings with him, however, I deeply suspect that he's unable and unwilling to be stretched at all. I honestly can't imagine him even being stretched by 2%. The man, then, was an example of a brittle person: a human soul petrified into something akin to opaque glass. Even as I write this, I'm trying not to judge him. Perhaps he's brittle and gruff because he's been through more harm than I can imagine. Perhaps it's the only remaining way to defend himself. Or maybe he's just tired of being stretched. Whatever the reason, he remains a difficult sort of person to aid.

If I can't stretch him, if I can't broaden his horizons and help him see the world in a new way, then everything I do will fall into one of two things. I will either tell him what he wants to hear, or I'll refuse to tell him what he wants to hear. The former choice will result in no change being done (not that that's automatically a bad thing), and the latter choice will result in nothing more than his indignation and maybe a few complaints my way. What else can I do for him, beyond merely listening? What else could my role as a priest be in his life? In short, all I can do is to hope that I stumble upon a spot in his mental shield, and find something that moves him beyond the ordinary matters of his life. After all, people always surprise me. Even the grumpy ones.

Chapter Two: Superstitions: Catholic and Otherwise

Do people take faeries seriously any more? It seems that people in the olden days
(whenever they were) believed in faeries, and they don't any more. But it's getting on for
650 years since Geoffrey Chaucer wrote that same thing. People have *always* thought
that faeries were something in which humans believed at some time in the unenlightened
past.

– *Changeling: The Lost*, Justin Achilli

There's a concern about Catholicism in general that comes up fairly often, that the
Catholic faith is little more than socially-acceptable witchcraft. The precise phrasing varies, in
my experience:

"Isn't Catholicism one part Christianity one part paganism?"

"The Church actively opposes science and modern technology."

"Catholics worship Mary and other human beings."

"Catholic Mass exhibits cult-like behavior, especially when everyone rises and kneels at the same time, or recites the same thing such as the Lord's Prayer."

"Catholic belief is polytheism disguised as monotheism."

I'm sure that there are many who would be able and willing to add to that list. Rather than deny it outright, my assessment is somewhere in the middle-ground: Catholics are approximately as superstitious as anyone else, and life goes on as always.

To be sure, Catholics have some silly traditions and habits, and at least a few may be justifiably labeled as "superstitions." To the best of my knowledge, Catholics are really the only Christians who are known to bury a statue of Saint Joseph in their front lawn. A "Saint Joseph Home Selling Kit" can be purchased on amazon.com for under $8.00. The ritual involves burying a small statue of Joseph upside down when one wishes to sell their home (or other property). The idea is that Joseph will help you sell the house and provide a buyer to you; when the property is sold, you dig him up and let him out. Armed with mere common sense, there are plenty of concerns to be had. First, strong-arming Jesus' dad is no way for any Christian to behave. Second, the link between real estate and Saint Joseph is tangential at best. Third, one could assume that an angry and uncomfortable Saint Joseph would sabotage the seller's efforts, rather than help them. And lastly, there remains the simple and direct argument that there is no sensible reason to believe that such a private and quasi-spiritual action would have any bearing whatsoever on earthly and financial matters between people. After all, if people possess free will, how could Saint Joseph influence the sale?

The straightforward example of Saint Joseph statues is an appropriate introduction to how superstition remains a part of modern Catholic life, in spite of any predictions to the contrary.

14

Indeed, I imagine that most people consider themselves at least somewhat reasonable and assume that the future would gradually have less and less superstition in the daily lives of average people. Such a thought is also reflected in this chapter's opening quotation. Regardless, superstition remains in the world today, and in no small quantity.

Of course, superstition is a word that involves a reasonable amount of overlap with other concepts. For the purpose of this chapter's focus, the universal presence of superstition is not a question of either ritual or tradition. A given action can indeed be a superstitious and traditional ritual, all at the same time. Further, as I make the argument that all people have at least some superstition in their lives, the same could be said for ritual and tradition. However, for the sake of clarity, it's all about superstition for now. Ritual can be thought of as repeatable and purposeful action (such as prayer, or getting coffee before starting one's workday), and tradition is that which is handed down (such as specific family holidays, home remedies, or a precise way to organize photos and documents). As both of those concepts have less stigma attached to them, we can leave them alone for the time being. Superstition is more deserving of some critical thought and reflection.

Perhaps, to better evaluate it in daily life, we ought to rewind a bit and examine the exact definition of the word "superstition". According to the Catechism of the Catholic Church,

"Superstition is the deviation of religious feeling and of the practices this feeling imposes. It can even affect the worship we offer the true God, e.g., when one attributes an importance in some way magical to certain practices otherwise lawful or necessary. To attribute the efficacy of prayers or of sacramental signs to their mere external

15

performance, apart from the interior dispositions that they demand, is to fall into superstition" (CCC, paragraph 2111)

Naturally, that is a very fine definition of the word. It boils down to the idea that the practices and belief of superstitions unreasonably focus upon external signs at the expense of authentic faith. The Church may be rightly concerned with superstition, therefore, as superstition may fully arise from Catholic practices as easily as rituals entirely unique to anyone in the Church. I wish to offer an alternative definition for the rest of this chapter, and for one reason alone: one may very well read the Catechism's definition and falsely conclude that it does not apply to them. After all, if a person professes no religious faith of any kind, then the sin of superstition is not likely to be seriously considered. However, the original point of this chapter remains: all people have the potential to fall into superstitious practice, whether they realize it or not.

To that end, I offer an alternative definition of word, this time from the *Collins English Dictionary*: "a superstition is an "irrational belief usually founded on ignorance or fear and characterized by obsessive reverence for omens, charms, etc." This is the understanding of superstition that concisely cuts to the universal core of the problem (without contradicting the definition of the Catechism): a superstition must have some direct connection with ignorance or fear, no matter which characteristics it is expressed with.

Imagine a high school freshman, newly arrived at their school at the beginning of the year. Now imagine that student acting fearful of their upcoming experience due to rumors they've heard about the school's bullies and/or intimidating teachers. They sneak from one class to another, attempting to go by unnoticed, and they fail to make friends due to their constant effort

16

of avoiding unwanted attention. After some time, this student comes to understand that the rumors were largely untrue and high school isn't as bad as it once seemed.

Now imagine that same freshman, with the same behavior in school. Only now, they are not acting on rumors but direct threats they received throughout the summer. As they go about the day-to-day activities of high school life, the summer threats fail to become a reality. In fact, after a few weeks, it turns out that the true senders of the summer threats were not members of that school and were caught and punished well before the school year began. They will not be a part of the student's life in any way from here on out.

The first scenario could be termed superstitious: baseless fear was the primary cause of the student's behavior as they began the school year. The second scenario, by contrast, could not be fairly termed as superstitious behavior. With direct threats in play, there was more than simple fear at work in the student's behavior. Rather, there was a credible concern for one's safely and well-being, even if fear remained a part of the equation. For the student of the second example, facing down fear was only one part of the solution: the threatening individuals would need to be dealt with as well (even if my example involved a somewhat extreme resolution).

The point here is that being superstitious is not the same as being wrong. People think incorrect things all the time while still being reasonable individuals. Our failure to perfectly analyze facts into accurate conclusions is a part of life, and mistaken ideas themselves are not reason enough to look down upon someone as a person. Superstitious people may indeed make errors of judgment or reason, but non-superstitious people can be equally in error at any given moment. Just ask a Republican about the Democratic Party's errors of judgment. Oh, and don't worry if you can't find an appropriate Republican to speak with. A Democrat detailing the errors of the Republican Party will literally serve my point equally well. The errors and contradictions

17

that pepper people's thoughts every day in every corner of the world is not, strictly speaking, superstition.

With respect to people acting out on their beliefs, a superstition is, simply put, the illusion of causality. The subject undergoes action A, the object undergoes action B, and the superstitious mind connects actions A and B by something more than mere coincidence. This illusion of causality has its roots in ancient philosophic thinking, for fans of classic thought processes and/or Latin. This particular definition of superstition is summed up in the phrase "post hoc ergo propter hoc", or "after this, therefore because of this". Also termed the "post hoc fallacy", the phrase concisely illustrates the absurdity of connecting one event to another due to their chronological order alone. More even so perhaps than fear, this ignorance of true and direct causal connections (in favor of simple but ultimately incorrect ones) can create more superstitious beliefs than we give it credit for.

I am not at all convinced that there is *anyone* in the world that is completely immune to this sort of thinking. I can illustrate this point by three experiential case studies, and none of them involve Catholics.

Case Study #1: Brittany the Dog

To begin with a simple disclaimer, I never considered our family's cocker spaniel Catholic. I know that some people declare that the family's religion is at least partially spread to pets, but Brittany never went to Mass with us and to the best of my knowledge she was never baptized or went to confession. Perhaps one day I'll write a second edition of this little book, complete with a copy of a puppy baptismal certificate.

Back in high school, perhaps 1996 or 1997, we celebrated the 4th of July at our house. There were friends and family present along with a bunch of neighbors. The sun set and my dad brought out the big box of fireworks to set off. As there were plenty of younger children present, we all got to enjoy the simple pleasure of pretty lights and sparks without feeling ashamed. Now, these fireworks were almost exclusively fountains - one of the few types of legal fireworks available for purchase in Wisconsin. Fountains are silent or nearly-silent fireworks that spray a shower of sparks for a minute or two. They're colorful, relatively safe, cheap, and a reasonably sized box will last for a good hour or so. The adults didn't really care, because there were too many children around for the more dangerous ones anyway.

Well, the one living thing around that hated these things was our dog Brittany. Although "eating human food or human valuables" was her greatest pleasure in life, "barking at things" was a close second. As soon as the first firework went off, she ran full speed toward the sparking and hissing box in the backyard. For the entire duration of the fountain's little show, she barked her little heart out while being showered in sparks and smoke. Naturally, no one was willing to get her and pull her back because of the sparks. However, sure enough, the sparks died down and the firework was expended. At that point, Brittany trotted victoriously back to the family with singed and smoking fur. You could almost see the pride in her eyes: she successfully defended the family against a malevolent and dangerous object, monster, predator, enemy, or whatever she regarded it as. From that point on, Brittany then knew that if she barked long enough at strange lights, they would eventually go away. This simple fact in the mind of Brittany was evident that whole night long, as the dog continued to bark ferociously at every firework we lit - at least until we put her in the house for her own safety. Even after that night,

19

Brittany had a knack for barking whenever something unknown came around, and she had total confidence that her bark would eventually overcome any obstacle.

Obviously, this first case study is tongue and cheek. There are profound differences between an animal's natural reactions and a human being's superstitions. Dogs bark at unknown objects and new sounds, no matter the specifics. Even so, Brittany's experience with those fireworks can serve as a learning opportunity. Brittany, understandably, failed to distinguish between causality and correlation. Superstition is in part exactly that: the false assumption of causality: the Church's definition as well as the Collins dictionary definition both support this ultimate and critical point. Correlation is not causation, although many people witness the former and assume the latter. Some philosophers, like David Hume, would state that no one can ever truly prove causality. Still, some instances of causation are more obvious than others. We all have harmless little assumptions in life, and sometimes we're mistaken. When that happens, we learn from it and we grow. By contrast, when we allow our superstitions to become harmful, we become a bit more like Brittany on the 4th of July: the dog who was convinced that barks could scare fireworks away. Her burnt and patchy fur was testament enough to the harm that came to her as a result.

Case Study #2: Gamers

I am a gamer to the very core of my being, and I am proud to call the closest of my friends gamers as well. Although gamers have a great many subgroups among them, I consider myself a gamer generalist with leanings toward tabletop games and LARPs (Live Action Role-Playing Games). That means that I favor the games that favor storytelling over games with an outright winnable objective; I play to have fun, rather than to compete. Still, I count among my friends the nerds, geeks, gamers, and sci fi/fantasy enthusiasts that come in all shapes and sizes. Generally speaking, this demographic enjoys a number of commonalities. Gamers tend to be well-educated and intelligent people, and often go on to do great things in life. Gamers tend to keep in contact with one another, if only sporadically, and they usually maintain a sense of child-like wonder. For these reasons and more, I suspect that gamers are substantially happier than the people around them. Finally, there is a strong tendency among gamers to be logical, reasonable, and empirical. Therefore, an average gamer will not be terribly religious, and will highly value a scientific outlook on life. That said, one would suspect gamers to be remarkably insulated from superstitious habits! With that perfectly understandable conclusion, I must regretfully disagree.

While in college, the four years of my life when I gamed the most and interacted with fellow gamers the most, I had the pleasure of playing with a great many people in a variety of settings. Most superstition among gamers comes down to the dice - which most games use to a greater or lesser degree. Gamers will purchase (with their typically limited supply of money) dice purification kits to keep their die roll high. A friend of mine asserts to this day that he rolls well when the dice are somehow on the color green. Gamers will roll their dice in specific ways when an important result is required, and touching another person's dice is considered a profoundly rude and impolite act. After all, who would want their dice to be corrupted by another person's aura/karma/luck stat/whatever-you-want-to-call-it?

Of course, there is a fair counter-argument to include here. So far, one could respond to the above instances as things gamers simply do for humor and fun. After all, gaming is recreation, and recreation should never be taken too seriously. So what if tabletop gamers have a series of harmless rituals with respect to dice? To that I say "fair enough," apart from one final concern. Gamers have superstitions and rituals, and they are not always held in a spirit of amusement or casual enjoyment. Sometimes, gamers do silly things with complete and total fury and rage. When gamers lose a major challenge specifically due to a poor die roll, they will angrily punish the dice themselves. Common punishments include gargling the dice in one's mouth (my favored technique), throwing them in the garbage, or even flushing them down the toilet. The idea, by-and-large, is that such an act will teach the remaining dice to fall in line and perform better. It is not unlike the stern discipline technique of a Roman legion, termed "decimation", where a poorly performing unit will have 10% of its men beaten to death by the other 90%. Of course, any sensible person would tell you that such a monstrous act of cruelty cannot possibly have any effect on an inanimate object like a set of dice. And yet, these practices most certainly continue in suburban basements and college dorm lounges the world over!

Case Study #3: Nurses

My third and final case study with respect to the prevalence of superstition is founded upon a bastion of science and rationality, sustained by a true desire to help other people: the hospital. Although my personal experience will only involve one hospital in particular, I have been assured that my observations can be easily found in practically any other medical institution. For a ten-week period in the summer of 2012, I served as an intern hospital chaplain. This was a part of my training as a seminarian, and I really loved my time in that place. Well, I was assigned to a particularly challenging unit early on: I was given a medical/surgical unit, pediatrics, and the pediatric ICU. The pediatric ICU was the only Intensive Care Unit that would be given to a brand-new chaplain such as myself. Part of the reason for the exception is that a typical pediatric ICU is a small unit and would not take up a great deal of a chaplain's time on average. So while my time was divided between three different units, the pediatric ICU was my most cherished department. I knew the nurses there better than most, and I was able to develop a stronger relationship with the patients and families who were in the hospital for a greater length of time. I would like to think I was welcomed and appreciated there, as well.

Now, I was fairly fortunate during my time - we had a below-average rate of disaster and death for that overall ten week period. I was even more sheltered than that personally: days when I worked were strangely calmer and quieter than others. We had a running joke that if Chaplain Justin was on call during the night, no one would be in grave danger. But the shift after mine would inevitably have twice as much tragedy. It was honestly an odd thing for the chaplain department to observe, especially near the end our time together.

Anyway, near the end of my service, I found myself hanging out with the nurses of the pediatric ICU with nothing especially important to do right that second. After a little while, our conversation started to involve a breakdown of the unit's rooms. See, the unit only had eight rooms or so, and two were almost never used. I recall the pediatric ICU had an average of three patients at any one time. I listened to the nurses unanimously agree on the essential points:

"Yes! That's absolutely true! Room two is the long stay room. Patients in room two are normally here for a while."

"And that would make room three the drama room, where families fight all the time for one reason or another."

"So room four is the short stay room, obviously."

"Right."

"And, obviously, room one is the death room."

It was at this point that I foolishly chose to enter the conversation. "Well yeah, but we haven't had a death here in a long time, right?"

"Why on earth would you say that? What is wrong with you? Shut up, right now, and never say that again!"

It was pretty scary about how quickly they all turned on me. I apologized and rushed out of the unit with as much dignity as I could manage.

Now, in my defense, I was correct. We had not had a child die in the unit for about a year, give or take a month or two. I figured that was a fact worth celebrating, or at least taking a measure of pride in as a hospital. However, such things are *not* said out loud. The nurses saw my question as tempting fate, as if my words would lead to a child's demise in the immediate future. After I bought some apology chocolate for the entire unit staff, and after a genuine apology and promise to never say such a thing again, we got back to our old working relationship. They knew that I meant no ill will, and all was well from then on. However, I never forgot how much distress I caused from my one simple statement of fact: those hospital employees were abhorred by me in that moment! That superstition of silence was not something that was a source of amusement, or a way of dealing with a stressful career. It was something a bit more sacred than that - it was an unspoken understanding between them all that such things shall not be said. It was serious, it was not up for discussion, and it certainly was not an optional rule for know-nothing chaplains such as myself.

I, for one, remain grateful that I learned that aspect of hospital subculture early. It serves me well as a priest who visits hospitals rather frequently. Patients, family members, and hospital workers alike have discomforts about sensitive topics. Even if I come to anoint someone on their deathbed - someone hours away from death - I may not have the freedom to talk about death.

While that strikes me as odd and a symptom of denial, I cannot disobey such wishes. If a family cannot hear about death at that time, it is not my place to force it upon them. I do what I can, and I mentally prepare to see them again when they come to me with a different set of basic spiritual needs. I have come to see this as one part of the grieving process: people will talk about death when they are good and ready. If the hospital is not the place for such a discussion, so be it. The very institution of a hospital surely discourages such talk, and the reasons for that are legion and far too large for the scope of this particular book. However, perhaps that systematic distancing from the reality of death is what I experienced that day in the pediatric ICU...

For Brittany's case study, I clarified that the example was imperfect due to the difference between a dog's thinking and a person's. For the case studies of gamers and nurses, there is another disclaimer that deserves to be stated: the above mentioned superstitions are almost something automatic or subconscious in nature. What if I approached any of the people in the stories above, twisted their arm, and asked them point-blank if they really believed in these practices of dice cleansings or death talks? I am sure that every single one of them would say "no, of course not". Who would genuinely defend the reasonableness of anything stated in those two case studies? This is the link to the chapter's initial quote: superstition is something that survives longer than anyone could reasonably expect, because superstition is something that happens in between our more reasonable and rational moments. Superstition origins have wide spectrum of possibility, from defense mechanisms to silly traditions meant to amuse. This is not a bad thing most of the time. Rather, this is something that gives flavor to human existence.

With the three case studies above in mind, I see a baseline level of odd behavior and local custom in *all* people. The odd behaviors I happen to witness probably have very little empirical or objective value, and that is alright in the long run. There may very well be people who honestly have no such rituals or patterns of thought in their daily lives, and I suppose I can offer my congratulations to them. For the rest of us, as we live our lives with a certain measure of silly customs and/or unfounded fears, the key may be simple respect.

Rather than criticize and mock each other when our little superstitions come to the surface, maybe we can see a bit ourselves in such behavior. Who knows? If we can manage that, we might just have greater focus to tackle the real problems and challenges in front of us and continue to cut away all that sicken us and truly keeps us from being the people we're meant to be: drugs, violent impulses, hatred, prejudice, and cruelty. I, for one, refuse to equate any of those things with the simple acts of burying a statue in front yard, flushing dice down a toilet, or refusing to speak of death while at work. We are all silly and odd people much of the time, and we can afford to celebrate and accept that. In fact, we can even manage to do that while still striving to improve ourselves and better understand the world around us.

Chapter Three: Talks of Faith, Peace in Church, and All the Difficulty in Between

Looks like you've lost control

Somethin' goin' on in your soul

I can see you comin' from a mile away

Savin' the day, savin' the day

When you get to the point where it's drivin' you insane

-"Savin' The Day", by Alessi, *Ghostbusters OST*

When people meet a priest who's brand-new to the ministry, general curiosity often prompts them to ask one of two questions:

1. What's it like being a priest?

2. How do you enjoy being a priest so far?

These questions ought to be quite familiar to anyone who's begun a new job, moved to a new part of the world, or otherwise begun a new phase of their life. A friend of mine from Peace Corps, a couple of months before returning to the US, told us that he was prepared for the inevitable conversations that awaited him from friends and family back home. Whenever anyone asked "How was Africa?" he would simply answer, "It was hot and there were a lot of black people." At first, it seemed like a silly thing to say; a cheap joke at best. However, after dwelling upon it for a while, I came to realize that the sheer brevity of the answer was subtly profound. My friend's response could be considered a non-answer, in that it provides absolutely no real information about his time overseas. "How was Africa?" is a question that is too big to possibly be adequately answered. How could anyone summarize two years of foreign service on another continent without an hours-long talk complete with pictures and visual aids? Sometimes a quick and pithy answer is the only one that works: the tiny answer reflects the massiveness of the question.

"How do you like being a priest?" Like my friend from a decade earlier, I have my stock answer ready to go: "I love talking to people about faith and things that matter, and I am at peace in church. And it's everything in between that drives me crazy." In truth, I knew this would be my answer before priesthood, because it is largely how I described the five years I spent in seminary. It was a slightly different answer: "I enjoy my classes, and I'm at peace in church. And it's everything in between that drives me crazy." All three segments of my answer can be expanded upon.

"I love talking to people about faith and things that matter." As a parish priest, I no longer spend a great deal of time in a classroom. However, the part of my mind that enjoys the act of learning for its own sake is the same part that loves teaching as well as learning from all the people that I share my life with. Most of the time, the highlight of my day or week is a meaningful conversation with someone who has sought me out for one reason or another. These conversations could be private confessions, counseling sessions, sincere talks over a meal or a cigar, or a relatively brief exchange in a hallway or breakroom. When two people share ideas with one another with respect and trust, only good things can happen. Both people gain - both people have the opportunity regardless of which was the more knowledgeable or experienced person. This phenomenon can happen in groups, to be sure, but the greatest potential in my life has always been within a one-on-one exchange. There is power in trusting one specific person with an idea, value, or belief that you hold dear to your heart. Likewise, there is power in receiving such trust. This is a healing power more than anything else. It is a way, available to us all, to refresh and restore our faith in humanity and in one another as individuals.

One cool thing about being a priest is that people will approach you when no one else can help them. Priests often find themselves in conversations where respect and compassion can undo years or even decades of continual despair or isolation. Of course, that very act of caring and listening is a skill that belongs to us all - some of us simply utilize it more often than others.

Take note: I did not feel comfortable with "talking to people about faith". In reality, it is "talking to people about faith *and things that matter*". Faith is, naturally, a topic priests are eager to discuss. However, it does not stop there. When people share their passions and interests (and pains) with me, that same power of healing is as present as if we were discussing advanced spiritual experiences. Even if people do not realize it, when they are free to express their love for their interests, they are indeed growing toward God and righteousness. It comes down to truth.

Discussions with my Jewish friends regarding kosher law are as edifying as Catholic debates about the anointing of the sick. When I talk to young adults having difficulty with their religious education, they are often timid and reserved until we find some sort of common ground. Once that common ground is met and we have an incredibly geeky conversation about books or movies, the rest of the talk is an absolute breeze for both of us - as if their extroverted twin took their place while my back was turned.

Those moments of mutual understanding are priceless. Even if we largely ended with a glum conclusion, such as a teen dropping out of their confirmation program, it is easy to walk away from the conversation feeling the presence of God's grace. Mutual understanding and respect belong to the Holy Spirit, and such efforts cancel out a multitude of sins. Anyone with a love for conversation and a willingness to learn from others most certainly has a skill to offer up to ministry - be it priesthood or otherwise. If done reasonably well, it will sustain your spirit in the midst of your other challenges and difficulties.

In another sense, "I love talking to people about faith and things that matter," applies to seminars, workshops, classrooms, and small group discussions. While I certainly favor one-on-one talks when possible, teaching moments are valuable when any number of people are present. Two specific contexts come to mind: formally teaching children at my parish's grade school, and a two-day suicide prevention workshop that I attended in California. Both thankfully generated and/or maintained a profound sense of solidarity; I feel a greater connection with humanity because of efforts and experiences like these. That solidarity is the result of two or more people sharing their faith or the parts of their lives that truly matter to them.

Teaching a thirty minute religion class at the grade school level is an experience without any real comparison - it is different from any other subject, as it is the middle ground between objective fact and subjective opinion. On second thought, I suppose it might be compared to a mix between speech class and history class. It is a thirty minute period with a degree of objective information (and dare I say, a few things worthy of memorization!), as well as a degree of discussion, exploration, questioning, and doubt. I rarely had a day where my lesson plans were followed exactly, and most of the time I did not mind at all. The important elements for a priest teaching in the school are easy enough to meet:

1. Make time to go in the first place, and reinforce the fact that the kids are worthy of your time and effort. Far too many priests are willing to cancel their school visits for an emergency meeting. Soon enough it becomes habit.

31

2. Give the kids a chance to ask their questions. They won't always have them, and plenty will be silly and relatively pointless, but they are worth hearing and answering to the best of your ability.

3. Teach them parts of the faith that you care about and have enthusiasm for. Priests who have the ability to teach in their schools will do so as a secondary ministry - priests who teach full time do so at the college level. As such, we cannot teach children everything they need to know, and we need to put our faith in the teachers, parents, godparents, and other role models to get that information to them. However, if we are going to effectively supplement that process, we need to do so in a way that the students respond to. Enthusiasm and genuine interest are the very best start to doing exactly that.

As a wrap-up thought regarding my teaching time, these three pieces of advice are equally applicable to parents who would like to take a more direct role in their children's education. Parents are often welcomed by teachers with open arms as impromptu guest speakers... A parent who takes the time for their kids in school will most certainly have that effort noticed, and it is a very positive effect overall. That same parent, by virtue of a different learning environment than at home, can really get a class's attention with a bit of preparation. Once a parent has the class's attention, the stage is set to do some real good in the lives of the kids. Just one clear and helpful message can echo in those kids' lives for decades to come.

Where those teaching efforts were more-or-less a regular part of my week, the suicide prevention workshop was a one-time effort over two days. The workshop itself was fantastic, and I remain quite grateful that I chose to attend it. I recommend such an event to anyone with a degree of counseling experience. Those of us at the conference with backgrounds of social work, religious ministry, or psychiatry excelled at all parts of the training. By contrast, the attendees who were correctional officers seeking to reduce the risk of suicide in jails and prisons had a harder time. They benefited from the session involving the warning signs, but less so from the sessions involving interpersonal communication skills.

For all that the workshop offered me in terms of concrete information which was directly relevant to my vocation and ministry, it was something else entirely I remember the most fondly. The two most meaningful hours to me, of the entire workshop, was the getting-to-know-each-other talk. Everyone recognized the activity: a bunch of strangers get their chairs into a circle and the group leader starts an ice breaker to get everyone talking. Everyone shares their name, home city, and something interesting about themselves (or their favorite movie, or what they would normally be doing at this time of the week). The questions rarely have much substance - they are excuses to get people talking, and the system normally works pretty well.

Well, our time in the chair circle was a bit different than a normal ice breaker. Because the third question was very antithesis of a trite question. "Why have you come to this suicide prevention workshop, and what personal experience have you had with suicide?" Is it any wonder that twelve people took two hours to do an ice breaker?! We poured out our souls to one another that afternoon. Needless to say, no one was nodding off near the end and no one knew what the next person was going to say. I was in the minority: I was there for largely professional reasons with no experience of suicide by way of friends or family. Most of the group had a very personal and extremely emotional tale to tell. One lady, a social worker as I recall, shared the story of her divorce and the subsequent suicide of her husband. She sat there and explained to us, with tears in her eyes, about how she knew and believed that suicide was wrong... and yet she still felt genuine relief at her ex-husband's death. It was the sort of soul-bearing talk that can only happen with absolute trust and respect among all involved.

33

Another member of the group, a woman in her mid-twenties or so, explained her brush with suicide with far more ease than I would have imagined. In her case, the suicide prevention workshop appealed to her because she was suicidal at one time herself. Although she was far better than she had been, she still remembered her mental state of despair and emptiness while the suicidal thoughts were at their strongest. At the time of the workshop, she was engaged and well on her way toward becoming a counselor or social worker (forgive me, I cannot specifically remember which one). During her turn to talk, we all listened intently and sympathetically: we all seemed to know that we were in the presence of someone who had been to the absolute pit of human experience, yet managed to fight against those terrible emotions and regain control over her life. To a passive onlooker, she might appear quite ordinary or even sheltered and naïve. However, at the core of her being, she is a woman who knows how rough life can be, and she is a woman who has chosen to do something about – both for herself and for others in similar need. Where else could she share such information? Besides trusted friends and family, the opportunities must have been scarce at best. Yet our group ice breaker gave her the chance to speak about something that was truly important, knowing that she would be heard and at least partially understood.

When it was time to part ways and head home for the night, we all left with a certain glow about us. I felt like a bond had been formed between us, even knowing that we would be together as a group for a mere two days. That bond, forged with nothing less than the truth of our past experiences, made the next day's exercises all the more effective: it was easier for us to learn from one another, and I fully believe that it was mainly due to the trust and respect and honesty that we had between us as a group. That sort of genuine discussion is something of a cornerstone, with respect to the question of what priesthood is really all about.

"I am at peace in church." All-in-all, that's a pretty reasonable thing to expect a priest to say. However, it's a significant statement coming from me because I have grown into the joys of liturgy. Liturgy is a fairly common word in Catholicism at it simply means "public worship". Worship that somehow involves more than one person. Praying to God in your bedroom is not liturgy, it is simply prayer. Mass is liturgy, as is the Sacrament of Confession or a rosary group that meets in a coffee shop. The tricky thing about liturgy is that it needs to have rules and it needs to be predictable and understandable. After all, if multiple people desire to share a common experience, they need to all understand what is happening around them. Hence, liturgy cannot have too much improvisation or go too far off script. If the very people participating in liturgy are confused and lost, then very little good is being accomplished. The simple pleasure of a familiar ritual is a key ingredient to liturgy.

The significance of my testimony, "I am at peace in church," is this: I didn't fall in love with liturgy at a young age, which contributed to my priestly vocation. I fell in love with self-giving service and God's direct presence in my life: that is what led me to priesthood at the beginning. I might very well have become a priest with no real love for Sunday Mass or any other Sacrament. Of course, I pity any priest in such a state; a priest with no love for liturgy is a difficult priest to picture happy and content in life.

No, for me the process was somewhat reversed: I chose to enter seminary and seriously consider priesthood. As a direct result of that decision, I was exposed to greater liturgy in my daily life, and that liturgy proved to be a great joy beyond any earlier expectation.

Every so often, a friend of mine will give me a half-compliment: "Your life seems really great, Justin! I'd love to do what you do, apart from all the priestly things." In other words, they would love to be a priest minus Mass, Confession, funerals, and prayer. For them, the good parts of priestly life is the joy of being an appreciated member of community - one everyone knows and recognizes. They value my opportunities to get away for spiritual retreat and continuing education, and they envy the fact that I interact with all age groups and demographics. I can see where they are coming from, although those statements mainly serve to remind me that I do indeed love the "priestly" parts of my life. The parts that seem the most boring or tedious to others are the moments in life that sustain my entire mission in life!

Part of the reason this idea is worth writing down is that it is the only way I can even hope to explain my conviction that there is something more to the Sacraments and prayer than simple man-made ritual. Indeed, everyone has rituals in life. Drinking coffee after breakfast is a ritual. Listening to music on the way to work is a ritual. The way the family does laundry is a ritual. Rituals are everywhere, and the Mass is indeed another ritual.

Amen, amen, I say to you: the Mass is much different than folding laundry or watching a parade on the 4th of July! It is a ritual and so much more. I can say that with confidence and certainty because I (at least partially) know what else the Mass offers besides the ordinary pleasure of a familiar and repeatable act.

Of course, being "priestly" and "churchy" is more than Mass on Sundays. When I say, "I am at peace in church," I am referring to my anointing of the sick, hearing confessions, and my prayer life. They are every bit as priestly as Sunday Mass. Apparently, these priestly parts of life scare people away from priesthood. Now that I am fully in that life, I must say that such fears are largely unfounded. For the most part, such activities prove more enjoyable and rewarding than one might assume beforehand.

As a short illustration to this point, consider the underestimated act of confirmation preparation. Generally, confirmations are the privilege of the local bishops. Priests confirm people without a bishop present as an exception to the rule, albeit a fairly common exception. So most people confirmed at our usual age of seventeen by a bishop – normally as close as possible to Pentecost Sunday. When adults over seventeen seek confirmation, their parish priest typically guides them through the preparation process and confirms them at a daily Mass after receiving permission from the Diocese to confirm in place of a bishop. These processes, which span over the period of a few months or a year at most, are wonderful "churchy" moments. When someone approaches me, seeking to deepen their faith through the Sacraments, the good far outweighs the bad. The two of us talk about history, the Tradition of the Church, the joys and difficulties of life, and what the future might hold with the aid of the Holy Spirit. I've never walked away from such a conversation with disappointment or frustration. When people come together in good faith and with a desire to grow, a real sense of peace among us both is the result.

I truly believe that everyone should have someone "priestly" in their lives, whether they are Catholic or not. Everyone should have a trusted friend or colleague in life: someone they can go to for any reason, and someone they can share any problem or secret with. Everyone should be able to request honest advice from this person, knowing that the conversation will remain confidential. And everyone should feel free to be themselves around at least one person, without fear of ridicule or judgement. As a priest, many people come to me with exactly these expectations and needs. It is my honor to serve them in such a way; it is my honor and privilege to serve them to the best of my ability, free of judgement or pre-existing expectations. In return for their dependence on me, I can only pray that those people realize how deeply they have affected me in return, and how they have deepened my relationship with God. For instance, every good confession that I hear restores or refreshes my faith in humanity, and that is a gift that cannot be understated! Such confessions can be as frequent as one in ten, or as infrequent as one in one hundred. Whatever their frequency, their worth cannot be appropriately expressed with mere words. That, my dear readers, is the honest truth.

Of course, the true labor of priests has very little to do with the Sacraments and genuine interaction between respectful people. The exhausting work a priest must trudge through, for the sake of the parish at large, boils down to the necessary evils of "administration". "Administration", at least for me, refers to matters of human resources, fund raising and financial matters, personal disputes among the congregation, staff meetings, and paperwork. Nine times out of ten, when I drag myself into the office in the morning after Mass, it is because I have a lengthy meeting to attend or because someone is upset about one matter or another. These are the moments of my workweek that leave me crawling into bed at 9:00 PM with an urgent prayer to God that the next day might be better.

As per the chapter's title, these are the workweeks that seem to be the "in between" periods of a priestly vocation: the work that needs to be done between the acts of sacred liturgy and authentic connection shared between human beings united in truth and compassion. By comparison, that work must always appear insipid and shallow. After all, if you've made someone's life better by your very presence on a Tuesday morning, how could you possibly look forward to a Tuesday afternoon of signing checks and sending out emails? Perhaps that stark contrast is what priests such as myself find so unsettling: the fact that a priest's labors involve fantastic joys, heartbreaking tragedies, and endless hours of paperwork. After some time, the paperwork almost begins to feel optional or unnecessary, even if we know full well that such matters require our attention just as much as anything else.

One day in the office, in particular, serves as an apt example for all the ordinary challenges in between the more satisfying elements of typical priestly responsibilities. It happened to be a Thursday during the school year, so I would be teaching in the school for the bulk of the afternoon, with a Human Concerns meeting in the evening. This was also during a period of time where I was the only priest in the office, and therefore had a considerable increase in responsibility. On an average Thursday, I would take the morning for myself and work for the entire afternoon and evening. If I was lucky, I could spend a whole Thursday on teaching and preparing for the weekend's liturgies. On this particular Thursday, I had no such luck.

I came into the office that morning; I chose to forego my late start that day because I was behind on my lesson plans and some other office matters. I went up to my office and got to work. The simpler emails and phone calls were completed easily enough. However, once I rolled up my sleeves and started preparing for that afternoon's classes, my productivity slowed to a crawl. One of my office workers knocked on my door for a few minutes of my time: a concern had been raised the previous evening with a student and their parents, and I needed to be brought up to speed on what was to be done next. That was important business, and it was my responsibility to be aware of those developments. As such, that interruption was a justified one and not a problem.

Attempting to regain my focus and get back to my lesson plans, I got a phone call with respect to some funeral plans that really could not be ignored for long. The next steps for those plans were taken, and once again I returned to my lesson plans. Mere minutes later, I received a last-minute email with a new agenda item for that evening's human concerns meeting. Although agenda items ought to be submitted far earlier than that, there was a good reason for the delay and the matter couldn't realistically wait until next month's meeting. So out of necessity, the agenda was adjusted to take into account the new discussion topic, and sent out to those who would be present that evening.

With the remainder of the morning swiftly running out, and my first class beginning at 12:35 PM, I closed my door and made an oath to myself that my lesson plans would get my full attention from that point on. Murphy's Law prevailing once again, I received yet another knock on the door. Thankfully, this latest matter was one that could wait until the late afternoon, so we both made a mental note to make some time after school hours. I wrapped up my preparations, wolfed down a quick lunch, and headed off to the school (luckily on the same campus, so at least there wasn't travel time to worry about). After school let out, and I rewarded myself with a well-earned cup of coffee, I headed back to the office. The matter I put off that morning involved complications with baptism paperwork and was once again something requiring a priest's attention and instruction.

From that point, there were a few other small matters to wrap up in the late afternoon. I locked up my office, caught up on my prayers, made some dinner, and headed off to the conference room for the 90-minute-or-so Human Concerns meeting. At the end of the night after all was said and done, I was able to look back on that workday and conclude that I spend the entire day reacting to problems, catching up on work I ought to have completed days ago, or fulfilling responsibilities that must be met every week. It was far from a wasted day, and it was not without its enjoyable moments. Still, it was a day that featured very little sanctification, and those days can feel incomplete when compared to most others.

It can be hard to estimate how much time such administrative responsibilities take up in a priest's week, assuming that days like the Thursday described in the previous paragraphs are fairly uncommon. At some points, administrative responsibility is light and there remains time for more optional tasks or secondary projects. However, there have been weeks where I have turned down meetings or gatherings for the sake of my primary responsibilities. After all, a

Sunday homily deserves a fair chunk of time to be written and rehearsed. A Lutheran hospital chaplain once explained to me that Lutheran pastors strive to work for one hour per minute of their homilies. Therefore, an average homily by me would require about eight hours of preparation. I probably give about half of that time to my Sunday homilies, and less for the minor ones I give during the week. The risk of office life is that priests can become so busy with administration that they neglect the community's spiritual needs. Indeed, no priest would wish such a fate upon themselves. However, the decision to take a step back from the day-to-day operations of a church is not an easy one, and the slow descent to administrative hell is enough for me to imagine. Still, one can always strive to remain aware of time management, and keep the big picture of the parish's needs in proper focus.

Overall, this is one way that priesthood can be regarded in three distinct parts: communication where it is needed the most, leading people through the Sacraments as a spiritual leader, and the in-between labors that keep a parish functioning properly. All three have their pleasures; all three have their frustrations or challenges. In a way, priesthood is a juggling act where all three sets of responsibilities need to be given their time and attention. The juggling act of priesthood will have times of ease as well as times of difficulty, but all three portions of priesthood will be ever-present. Beyond such an analogy, little else can be said; from here, stories and descriptions ought to give way to experience and example.

Chapter Four: Priests of Every Size and Shape

If you're not getting answers, ask better questions.

–"Q", by Cartel, *Chroma*

At I begin this chapter, I've been a priest for about 16 months: it's early fall of 2015. This means that priests have been a normal presence of my life for seven years plus change. I came back from my Peace Corps service in Africa in 2008 and began to apply to seminary. I was in Saint Francis de Sales Seminary for five years, and ordained in May of 2014. As I came from a family of Casual Catholics, I did not interact much with the Church on a regional level. Casual Catholics are the demographic of churchgoers who typically attend Mass two or three times a month and lose absolutely no sleep over any missed Sundays. Thinking back on my childhood and adolescence, no one in my family went to confession apart from the days it was mandatory for our education.

With that in mind, 2008/2009 was the start of a new phase of my life. Prior to that application process, I knew three priests and one bishop by name. People who were religious by trade were not a significant presence in my life, apart from my parish priest. I knew no nuns, no monks or friars, and I attended very few church activities after I was confirmed in high school. Once I began my application to seminary, that rapidly changed. I met new priests every month or so, and that trend continues today. While I don't personally know all 200-or-so priests of Milwaukee, I call many of them friends or at the very least brothers and comrades. I also studied with several hundred other priests-to-be at Sacred Heart School Of Theology, most of whom studied for other dioceses across the nation.

Now that I have met a wide array of clergy from all aspects of life, I have come to understand that priests are most certainly *not* a homogeneous demographic. Indeed, priests are an amazingly diverse group of men all across the board. As Bishop Don Hying (currently of Gary, Indiana) once expressed while rector of Saint Francis de Sales Seminary, "How would all of us here possibly come together, apart from the call to priesthood?" Believe me, it was a fair question! We were all male (a straightforward similarity, by any means), we were all Catholic (as far as I could tell, anyway), and we were all at least considering the notion of becoming priests (or pretending pretty darn well, anyway). There was absolutely nothing else that we all held in common as a group. We were not all Americans; we were not all native English speakers; we were not of the same economic class; nor were we all Catholics from birth. Of course, those are all surface differences. A sharp, if somewhat argumentative, person might hear that out and respond, "Fair enough, but you all believe in the same things. *That's* what unites you!"

Well, that isn't an unfair assumption... I wouldn't take offense at such a suggestion. However, it is ultimately incorrect once those apparently similar beliefs are taken out of a Bible or textbook and into the daily life of a living breathing human being. We believe the same things, insofar as mandatory Catholic beliefs are concerned. We all believe in Jesus Christ, and the power of the Eucharist. However, the details of our individual beliefs (and how we live them out) are far more varied than I thought possible. The core beliefs of the Catholic faith, most of them summarized in the Nicene Creed, are the only constants among us that I can cite with any degree of confidence. Once the Nicene Creed has been covered, our values and worldviews becoming alarmingly dissimilar. Allow me to illustrate this understanding with two observations of priests who are essentially polar opposites to me.

The first observation in question was a part of my change-of-attitude with respect to my parish. Having been at Saint Francis Borgia Catholic Church for years before priesthood, I was rather fond of the people there, and I developed a certain degree of possessive affection for the congregation. The thought of "my parish" falling into the hands of an unworthy successor was enough to increase my blood pressure purely out of animosity. Looking back on that relatively early point of view (perhaps within six months of my ordination), I still can't say where my genuine concern for my parish ended and my fear of being replaced by some kind of priestly nemesis began. My mindset involved at least some care for the people's spiritual needs as well as some selfishness. In quiet moments of weakness, I fearfully imagined my replacement as a proud and narrow-minded man who worked tirelessly to undo all of the work that I accomplished before him. Within one year, my opinion had completely turned upside-down.

By the time I'd been at the parish for a year and a half, I had formally requested to be transferred to a new parish after two years' time instead of three. The parish's drama had been deeply affecting my mental health, and in addition to those personal reasons, I truly believed that the parish needed a new priest more than anything. Simply put, both the parish and I needed a clean slate. I reflected and discerned the events of the past year that led me to that point: the pain that was wearing me down on a daily basis, as well as the ways that I was failing my people. Somewhere in that process, I realized that I became comfortable with a polar-opposite priest taking my place. In fact, I began to grow comfortable with the idea of that stereotypical priestly nemesis taking over where I left off! I was aware of the upcoming class of priests to be ordained, and I had a pretty good idea of which guys would be in the running for Saint Francis Borgia. I pictured the combination of those guys and the dynamics of my parish, and I didn't mind it anymore.

A totally different priest would do the parish well, in fact. Where I was easy-going, they would be firm and no-nonsense. Where I took great offense, they might show more leniency. My relative ignorance of the liturgy would be corrected by their staunch and informed orthodoxy. Where I tended to focus on teaching and one-on-one pastoral care, they would focus on theology and devotionalism. Ultimately, I concluded that my parish had learned a great deal from me during my time there, and my well was running dry. Those very same people, therefore, did not need a new Father Justin. They needed a new associate pastor with different priorities, different strengths, and different mannerisms. Those are the differences that make change worthwhile, far more than the new shortcomings and weaknesses that inevitably come with new people. Regarding priest assignments and parish needs, there need not be such thing as a priestly nemesis at all.

To be fair, that was an observation that put my changing attitude into focus. Out of respect to those priests I had in mind to replace me, the specific details of our differences will remain unstated. However, those very sorts of details are partially what this chapter is all about. So the second personal observation of the chapter will make up for it.

This observation happened to occur during a fall priest assembly, which takes place over a morning and afternoon. Our spring assembly takes place over two and half days and is partially a social gathering where we can all touch base and share a bit about our lives. The fall assembly is shorter and more professional. We gather and listen to a speaker for the morning, have lunch, and then regroup for a question and answer session with that same speaker for the afternoon. So in a way, the fall priest assembly is a one-day event in the spirit of continuing education, complete with a concrete topic that involves a ministry that all priests are involved with. For this particular assembly, the topic was sexual sin and how best to pastorally approach the issue as a Catholic priest. The speaker of the day was a priest with a background in psychology. He spoke about sexual orientation, masturbation, sexual promiscuity, the nature of human sexuality, and how social media has affected the expression of sexuality of our culture. He addressed how best to approach the issue in the confessional, in private conversation, and how best to deal with these struggles in our own private lives. I found his entire talk extremely refreshing to hear from a priest: he never contradicted Church teaching, but also never dismissed the scientific conclusions of contemporary psychological and biological studies. His message was rather consistent with my own, and I left that seminar with a number of new tools for when I'd next find myself in those sorts of conversations.

As we broke for lunch, I joined a table with a few priests that I don't interact with very often. We began to eat our meal and we chatted about nothing for a few minutes, as often happens during cafeteria-style lunch gatherings. Before long, however, I opened the proverbial can of worms with the timeless question that practically screamed out "please rant your heart out at me."

With a naïve sense of innocence in my voice, I asked, "So what do you guys think of the speaker so far?"

While I was simply making conversation, the climate of the table changed in an instant. One of the other guys, older than me and remarkably more experienced, explained to me his extreme disapproval about the entire talk. He was insulted that our speaker never talked about the power of prayer, he was offended that the speaker did not condemn homosexuality, and was fully prepared to completely disregard the seminar's advice as soon as he got back to the daily routine of his parish. Thankfully, I saw the writing on the wall, and I was able to remain diplomatic and not argue with him - it was a fight I couldn't possibly win. As I sat there and listened to his response to my question, I was initially disappointed that my fellow priest was so stereotypically rigid in his devotion to the classic Catholic stance on sexuality and sin. If someone was afraid to confess some sexuality-related sin to a priest, they most likely had a priest like him in mind. As a matter of fact, I myself would not feel comfortable confessing a sexual sin to him - even anonymously behind a screen.

With the background of that lunch conversation and that priest in mind, here comes the whole point of this chapter, summarized in one sentence:

I know for a fact that the ultra-conservative reactionary priest I met at lunch that day is personally responsible for immeasurably good works and has fought against the forces of evil with greater success and ferocity than practically anyone else I've ever met.

It is true that I can't prove the second part of that sentence: I can only look at the facts of his ministry and conclude that he's done far more than most. However, even with that disclaimer, I trust that my point here remains a powerful one - this gruff old-timey priest is doing good work in his life, the best way he knows how. He gets results, and I sincerely doubt that my "good deeds scorecard" will be anywhere near his when I'm his age.

To be fair, I still feel the same sense of disapproval with respect to his stubborn refusal to allow science and psychology to blend with his faith. That point of professional disagreement most certainly exists, and if I were to give him advice on how to be a better servant of God, that would be the overall point of my message. However, in spite of all that, I recognize that his style of ministry and his overall attitude has its place in the world. People *need* him, in the complete opposite way that people need me. A diversity of priests benefits a diverse set of parishioners. Thus, with the plurality of different people in need of one ministry or another, the Catholic Church does not need cookie-cutter priests. The Church certainly does not need 200 Father Justin Lopina clones. The Church needs one and only one of me, working alongside as many diverse and unique men of good will as humanly possible. The desire to serve and offer sacrifice, as best as one is able, mixed with a little bit of faith: the two ultimate requirements for priesthood. All other requirements either branch off from those two, or are expectations of no legitimate consequence. The bottom line of a true spirit of service, sacrifice, and faith will always and forever produce a brotherhood of priests, of every size and shape.

Chapter Five: The Liberation of

Being Counter-Cultural

Please remember that it's natural for a thing like me

-"Electricity Is In My Soul", by Steam Powered Giraffe, *Album One*

At the time of this writing, well into year two of priesthood, there is a very real perk to the job that continues to amaze me at all times. Now, and for the rest of my life, I am remarkably free from the more pesky expectations that the "real world" demands upon its denizens. I perpetually weep for a depressingly large percentage of my friends who find themselves mired in some of the more soulless conditions life has to offer. I have often literally cringed as I read Facebook posts of friends who woke up one day and realized that they were in crippling student debt in order to establish themselves in a career that they came to hate and despise. They didn't have the money or time to start over from scratch once again, and they didn't have the strength of spirit to remain. As the final insult, the jobs described in such posts never seemed to pay particularly well: these friends of mine never felt able to endure their job for 5 years, pay off their debt, and have enough left over for a new major or life transition. By God, as I read such reports, I pictured actual chains around my friends' wrists and ankles. It goes without saying that none of my friends deserve to feel that way. Never would I read or hear of such a thing and shrug my shoulders at their plight. Some plight is indeed man-made; we are responsible for a good chunk of our unhappiness when it comes around... but far too many people get trapped by a shiny promise with absolutely no weight of sincerity behind it. Through no fault of their own, the world around these people molds their lives in unwelcome and unwholesome ways. I've come to regard that effect as the "intimidation of culture": the summation of a given society's expectations taking precedent over an individual's personal well-being. In short, when a person conforms to a general norm at the expense of their central individual needs, they've fallen into this particular problem. For anyone like that reading this book, I hope and I pray that you find your way back to where you belong. A large portion of the world's intimidation of culture is imaginary. If you feel it pressing down on you, and you muster the courage to push back, you may well find that its strength is short-lived indeed.

How is priesthood counter-cultural, and why can I speak of this as if it no longer applies to me? Perhaps I should start with the most obvious thing and the part of the intimidation of culture that is not imaginary - money. When the world takes your money as well as your hope to make the money you need to get by, daily life can be a truly scary place. As a priest, I get to escape that particular problem in the very best way possible. I have work to do, and for that work, I'm paid enough money to get by, but not too much to be permanently distracted by wealth.

Now, priests aren't paid an absolute ton... but what we have goes a long way. We don't have families to provide for, we don't need big houses, we don't drive luxury cars, and we don't have all that much time to frequently visit Paris and Rome. We get invited to dinner often, so even our food budget gets stretched. Our pay goes to basic needs and student loans, and the rest can go to charities or other secondary expenses. It's an absolute blessing to be paid a moderate salary for good work!

So on one hand, I will never lack for money or basic needs. I will never go hungry, I will never be homeless, and I will never be denied basic health care. I have all the clothes I need, I have everything that I require in order to do my job, and I have absolutely no need to be competitive with my fellow priests. By that, I mean that there is no true benefit to being the priest with the fanciest chasubles (the garment we wear at Mass), the best car, or the most medallions blessed by Pope Francis. My worth as a priest has nothing to do with the things I own. That feels great!

On the other hand, I will never have too much money. Yes, having too much money can be a problem. So how much money is too much? The answer doesn't involve a precise amount. Rather, some people reach a point where having personal wealth and continually generating more personal wealth becomes a purpose in of itself, rather than what that money provides. Common parish priests don't really fall into that trap, at least not easily. We never build up the wealth one needs to forget what it means to have financial limitations. For that, I am also thankful. There are simple pleasures in life that I never want to be too good for. I never want to reach the point where I can't bear to sleep in anything but a fancy bed with softest mattress money can buy. I don't want to turn my nose up at dinners of ramen noodles or beans & rice (college food and Peace Corps food, respectfully). I don't want large HDTVs, or the newest model smartphone, or my own sailboat. I am content with what I have, and I see no reason for why I cannot continue to be content with this level of material comfort. The true joys of my life are immaterial, and by the grace of God, they will continue to be so for the entirety of my life. These immaterial joys include my friends, family, and the utterly inspiring stories found in my books, movies, games, liturgy, and Scriptures. I wonder how many of us stop and consider how fortunate we are in this day and age: we have an endless supply of tales to hear, and for the most part, they're all free or cheap enough for all to afford. That alone is a true blessing.

Beyond financial bliss, the act of living a true counter-cultural lifestyle becomes a bit more fluid. I don't mean "counter-cultural" as the opposite of what normal people do. I've never seen all that much value in that attitude, even during my high school years when I might have gotten away with that sort of thing. No, by "counter-cultural," I mean that to be empowered to live life as one see fit, without the fear of any sort of peer pressure or social stigma. Being molded by morality, ethics, laws, or values is one thing; being molded by peer pressure or social stigma is very much another. Looking back on my childhood, this attitude toward social stigma may have been the best indication that priesthood was always what I was meant for. I had always "marched to the beat of a different drummer," and I honestly cannot think of another vocation that would afford me this degree of freedom to live my life as I truly desire. Before I move on to specifics, know that I have my rules. I remain loyal to Church teaching; I maintain a lifestyle that honors the expectations of priestly excellence; and I still believe that there are actions that Christ always calls me to avoid to the best of my ability. However, those rules leave much for personal preference, and in the grand scheme of a human life, even the lifestyle restrictions and requirements of priesthood are negligible compared to the potential freedoms that are part of that same journey through life.

I have always loved dancing. It was a simple joy that was temporarily beaten out of me in middle school: such is life for shrimpy boys like I was. Unfortunately, that fear of embarrassment kept me from such things for the whole of my elementary school years and most of my high school experience. It was only in college that I was able to really enjoy dancing without fear of bullying or mockery. I went up from Beloit, WI to Madison by bus in order to join my friends for ballroom dancing during the weekend. Aside from a deeply rocky start, it became a real joy, and I regularly went back (alone or with fellow Beloit College students) for dancing throughout my undergrad years. As we neared the end of college, I bemoaned to my friend Heather (who had been my friend for six years, and visiting her was one of the biggest reasons I came to Madison for dancing) that I was still terribly awkward on the dance floor compared to her and others of our group. In essence, I felt that I was second-class. To this day, I remember Heather's response ringing clearly in my head. Heather stated, in no uncertain terms, that I would surpass her in no time at all. She reminded me that I tend to stick with things that I care about, and my ballroom technique would only improve over time as others would quit and chose to leave ballroom dancing behind. Naturally, I didn't believe her. It sounded utterly ridiculous and nothing more than a kind platitude to calm me down. However, no later than two years after that conversation, Heather's little prophecy came true. It came true and has never ceased to be true.

In every chapter of my life (which vary widely in both theme and setting), I have always found a way to interject dancing into my other tasks. I managed it in Madison, I managed it in Africa, I managed it in seminary (no easy task there), and I managed it in priesthood.

Although the pastoral value of dance is tangential at best, other esoteric interests of my personal life contain a practical advantage that is significant. For one thing, I have no fear of being judged for enjoying diverse media in my free time – from games to movies to books. I read all manner and age of literature. It is common to find me reading a paperback from 2013 in between the more challenging chapters of a non-fictional work from 1850. I can read philosophy as enjoyably as I read children's books. That is perhaps an overstatement: I occasionally have to give preference to the children's books on account of the fact that philosophic texts rarely have many entertaining pictures. I also love the fact that I own a smart phone and laptop and all that junk, and use it in my office right beside my quills, fountain pens, wax seals, and hand-written journals completed with sparkle pens of all different colors. It is healthy to mix the new and the old, and aside from an occasional chuckle, no one takes offense or shows concern over such matters. One's effectiveness toward others depends upon other more important qualities of character, such as a healthy sense of compassion and personal investment in the plight or suffering of those who are come calling for help. All priests do need to carry themselves with a certain degree of dignity - this is true. However, true dignity is not the same as living a boring life, and a genuine sense of one's interests and loves ultimately increases that idea of true dignity.

The second way my eccentricities help me is my above-average ability to connect with diverse people. I can minister to "average" people, due to being well trained in the tried-and-true ways of general ministry. However, I can also reach out with some success to various demographics – whether that demographic is the knitting committee or 4th graders. Of course, I am at my best when I'm with my fellow nerds, gamers, geeks, or sci-fi/fantasy fans. My first great connection as a clergyman, in the context of counseling, was when a teen came to me to talk about life in general and a few concerns she had. We talked for about an hour before she brought up the shows that she liked to watch. She was scared to bring it up, because they were programs her mother didn't approve of, and she assumed I'd look down on her for similar reasons. She sheepishly described a world where alchemy was real, and as she explained it, she clasped her hands together and then pressed them both palm-down on the table. I couldn't help but take a guess:

"Oh, are you talking about Full Metal Alchemist?"

"How did you know that I was talking about that show?"

"Well, for one thing, not too many shows involve alchemy. And you made the signature hand gesture. You might as well have said 'live long and prosper.'"

"But how do you know about the show in the first place? How do you know what Japanese shows are at all?"

From there, the conversation just burst into new life! We traded stories about our favorite Japanese animes and sci fi shows, and I gave her some appropriate advice about watching horror movies when such things came up between her and her mother. As soon as I revealed to her that I was a fellow fan of such media, we were both in a far better position to communicate with one another with enthusiasm and joy. It was a conversation to remember, indeed. Typically, a counseling session should be one hour or so. With her, we easily talked for two and a half hours. The professional side of my mind was screaming at me for breaking protocol, and tried to remind me of my other responsibilities (not to mention dinner) awaiting my attention. Still, I didn't heed that interior advice because the conversation with my parishioner was far too enjoyable and meaningful to end before its time.

I have had several connections like that - although none quite as surprising - as the months went by; every time the phenomenon occurred, I gave thanks to God for those seemingly random array of interests. For the people in my life who feel no real connection to a "typical priest," those interests become the bridge I require in order to do something truly good and helpful for another. To that end, I assert that no priest is a "typical priest" outside of the ones in seen in movies. All priests are men with unique and individual interests, and as a result we all have our favored demographic of people we prefer to minister to. While I believe that I am more diverse than the average priest in this way, it is nevertheless a reality that impacts us all and ought to be used to the greatest advantage possible.

In a more general sense than the above examples, there still remains the ability to appreciate life and beauty in a greater way than daily routines typically allow. This phenomenon is somewhat abstract and is difficult to put into words. The best I can do is to phrase it thus: from time to time, and without warning, I find myself entranced by something that utterly resonates with my very spirit. I would like to believe that everyone experiences this from time to time, even if they do not credit any spiritual worth to the matter. Haven't we all been stopped in our tracks by what is right in the world? Haven't we all had a moment where we remembered what an absolute joy a rainy night in summer is? Do we not remember the last time we were stunned by a true work of art, or puppies playing in the pet store window? I say that we all have moments when we discover something inspiring beyond words, and the very core of our being tells us "that thing is wonderful and the world is a little bit better than before". It doesn't need to be logical, or rationally explained. Sometimes, we bypass all of that and simply lose ourselves in the moment for no reason that we can immediately discern. The willingness to let yourself get lost in something unexpected and affirming – that is the true center of living a life that is unique and counter-cultural.

Chapter Six: The Monastery Experience, In Two Parts

Michael Palin: My old Dad used to say to me, 'Money doesn't buy you happiness.'

Eric Idle: 'E was right. I was happier then and I had NOTHIN'. We used to live in this tiiiny old house, with greaaaaat big holes in the roof.

Graham Chapman: House? You were lucky to have a HOUSE! We used to live in one room, all hundred and twenty-six of us, no furniture. Half the floor was missing; we were all huddled together in one corner for fear of FALLING!

Terry Jones: You were lucky to have a ROOM! *We* used to have to live in a corridor!

-"Four Yorkshiremen", Monty Python

At the time of this writing, I have experienced the setting and lifestyle of two monastic communities. One was a cloistered community of nuns in Denmark, WI - a few miles south of Green Bay. A cloistered community is where the monks or nuns are sealed away from the outside world, which is normally a lifelong commitment: the nuns in Denmark, WI were not permitted to be visibly seen by guests or visitors for any reason. The other was Saint John's Abbey in Collegeville, MN. I heard it said that all monasteries are entirely different from one another, and I am certainly inclined to agree with that. Allow me to begin with the Carmelite nuns of Denmark, WI.

I went with three other deacons and a priest for our "canonical priesthood retreat": a church-mandated get-away during the last year of seminary. It was one last period to think and pray before ordination to priesthood, free of any and all distractions. Of course, that last part is optional now. With cell phones and tablets, distractions are more common these days. Still, I made a good effort to be alone with God as much as possible. Here's the basic rundown:

-We were on retreat from Friday afternoon (three out of four of us left directly after final class at 5:00 pm) to Wednesday afternoon.

-There were four deacons (myself included) and Father John, the rector of the seminary.

-We were in a Carmelite convent which also featured a retreat center, which is fairly common of such places.

-We had more time together than usual: two prayer times, daily Mass, three meals, two or three sessions where Father John talked at us about something he deemed important enough to reflect upon, and finally a movie following dinner each night. I only made the time for one movie, so I don't recall the films the guys watched in my absence. However, Tuesday night's showing was *The Cardinal* (1963) and proved to be an excellent story to reflect upon with respect to priesthood. Allow me to add one more detail to that last point: his movies were two and half to three hours long - for each full day we were there. This means we had relatively little time to pray and/or rest, assuming that we participated in every provided activity. Oddly enough, I seemed to be the only one bothered by that. Luckily, at the start, Father John stated that we were free to do as we pleased: even skip a formation session and drive into town if we felt that we needed to get away in that manner. So I took Father John up on his offer: I skipped two movies and Monday's lunch and afternoon session. Monday was extremely fruitful in terms of praying and mentally preparing myself for the things life would be throwing at me in the years to come. My decision to go my own way was one I most certainly do *not* regret in the slightest.

-We had a retreat house with three rooms, and two separate rooms were in the convent proper. I got one of those rooms, with Father John on the far side of the chapel. This worked out perfectly: the other three wanted to be together, and I had greater need for isolated prayer, so it was reasonable for me to be the only deacon not sleeping in the retreat house. I had much more alone time than I would have otherwise, and I was about twelve steps away from the monastery's main chapel - the same one the nuns used.

My time resulted in some pleasant but forgettable times of rest, as well as a few remarkable memories from that time in the monastery in Denmark. The first and strongest comes down a renewed appreciation for silence and the dynamic between total silence and sung prayer. In various media, assassins, thieves, ninjas, and other stealthy characters often train at monasteries. I now understand the cliché of the monastery training montage: there is a profound and deep quiet to this sort of place which can be initially overwhelming. When we all first entered the chapel for a moment upon arrival, I was awed by the majestic quiet of the space. Later that first night of my retreat, around 9:30 PM or so, I had another chance to go to chapel on my own. Little did I know the nuns were in the middle of night prayer, which apparently went from 9:00 to 10:00. None of them could see me, or vice versa, as this was a strict Carmelite convent: as mentioned above, the nuns were cloistered from the world in a very real sense. While emergency services could enter the monastery, for instance, they were to have no ordinary contact with the outside world, and that included guests using their chapel. They resided in one part of the chapel, with others permitted to enter two guest wings. The space was specifically designed to block line-of-sight between the nuns and the guest areas. A priest (and his altar servers) would be able to see them while presiding a Mass; that was the only exception to this remarkably important rule for their way of life.

In a sense, you could think of the chapel as a large capital "T". The nuns remained in the lower part of the vertical dash, the guest wings were the ends of the letter's horizontal dash, and the altar was at the point of intersection. The nuns and guests were kept apart by gates and a large metal barrier. Each guest wing had a small two-foot-high gate that divided the sitting area from the sanctuary, which is the area immediately surrounding the altar. Generally speaking, the sanctuary should only be entered by people who have a reason to be there: priests, servers, or people distributing communion. So while it's not a sin to walk into a sanctuary, it is somewhat disrespectful. The small gates in the monastery chapel appropriately kept people from getting too close to the altar without reason, and therefore never had line-of-sight to the nuns at the bottom of the capital "T".

If the simple lack of line-of-sight wasn't enough to deter people, there was also a floor-to-ceiling metal fence between the altar and the nuns' segment of the church. I spent perhaps a total of an hour or two simply staring in wonder at that unique design decision. Who builds a giant "DO NOT ENTER" barrier in the middle of a church? Perhaps the nuns have the only reasonable answer to such a question: "people who highly value their private and sacred space, which their lifestyle depends upon." Needless to say, it was a fascinating place to be, and I would have taken it for granted if I was not alone to take in the environment in all its peculiarity.

Getting back to that first night with the nuns in the chapel, I walked into the appropriate guest space, which was totally silent. But a moment after I sat down, the nuns continued their readings and sung responses. By dumb luck and/or bad timing, I came in while the nuns were having a moment of silent reflection. I was embarrassed to have interrupted: it sounded like every step I took echoed throughout the entire space. And from that point in time, every single thing I did made noise. I used the kneeler, and it creaked louder than any other kneeler in recorded history. I could hear the stiff paper of my book creak and crackle as I turned the page. An accidental breaking-of-wind, no matter how minor, would be death sentence. When I decided to head back to my room, I tried with all my might to be silent and slip away without sound. I failed every test of agility, even the simple act of covertly walking away. Every single step I took was like a tiny boot stomp, all the way back to the outer doors. Now, I have always considered myself on the stealthy and quiet side, so the inherent noisiness of my existence greatly bothered me. Mind you, I didn't burst into tears, but it was an unwelcome surprise.

Three days later, I did much better. I slipped into the chapel before the nuns got there, silently opened and closed my book, raised up the kneeler during a particularly loud verse of a song, and soundlessly slipped away at the end! I'm not exactly sure what I did differently, but I managed to step without making any noise to echo throughout the chapel. It was kind of a fun little training exercise in being stealthy. So take it from me: monasteries and convents are the places to go if you wish to learn how to be quiet unnoticed. After the progress I made in one week, I must conclude that those nuns were superhumanly stealthy. Perhaps when we see or hear a nun, we are merely seeing and hearing what they allow us to? Of course, if that conclusion is correct, how would we be able to verify or prove it?

On the note of training, I chose to push myself physically as well as spiritually during this time. Besides some simple room exercises, I went on three outdoor runs: one per full day, with Monday as a rest day. According to my car, it was about twenty degrees Fahrenheit when I ran around the 2:00 - 3:00 PM range. And while my runs were merely 20 minutes, they were a tough 20 minutes. I didn't own winter running gear, and the snowy roads weren't very reliable when it came to traction. Still, it was a pleasure to get outside, play some music, and explore the area around the convent. I had some trouble breathing near the end due to the low humidity and temperature, and my fingers were aching from the elements, but overall it was time well spent. Naturally, I was imagining that this was all part of the ninjapriest training. After all, do not the Bene Gesserits from *Dune* (by Frank Herbert) teach us that human beings can surpass any pain?

One other thing worth reflecting upon is the sheer holiness of the space. I can sometimes be picky about things such as ambiance, and this chapel was exactly what I needed. It was quiet and beautiful, with a true serenity. I was surprised to feel such respect for a space with which I had so little contact: most of the time, I need to "bond" with a place before I feel at peace there.

Of course, it wasn't just the chapel: the surrounding countryside and snows helped the sense of being apart from busy daily life (in a good way). I felt like I had what I needed to really sink my teeth into the most challenging issues I still had left to struggle with. And thankfully, I was able to do exactly that. Questions such as, "how the hell did I get to this point?", and "why do I feel like college and seminary were years spent in profoundly opposite ways?", got the time they needed and deserved. Now, as only three months remained until I was thrust into Real Life (as opposed to never-ending studies of the seminary), I was all set - mentally and spiritually. Quiet reflection helps with such transitions.

-The aftermath – the infinite hypotheticals of clever 6th graders:

That year, my teaching responsibilities amounted to forty minutes of teaching 6th grade, and forty minutes of teaching 7th grade. I absolutely loved teaching religion as a deacon (and later as a priest), because I wasn't bound to any syllabus or lesson plan. Their teacher had them for the other days of the week and was responsible for their mandatory lessons, and that left me free to beef up their education with whatever topic I liked. The freedom was nice: if I wanted to play a game, I could. If I wanted to go nuts on Scripture, I could. Or, as I came to amusingly regret this time, I could talk about life with my students. The week after my retreat, I went into class a spiritually refreshed man, and I was eager to talk to my students about the nature of a spiritual retreat as well as the uniqueness of a proper monastery. I started off just fine, and I got some useful information into their heads. However, that learning process came to a halt remarkably quickly.

I made the mistake of talking about how the nuns were physically separated from their guests. I described the chapel, as well as the 20-foot-high metal barrier. Think of it as a more solidly-built version of a chain-link fence. Although it certainly covered the entire width of the archway, it did not reach the ceiling. Rather, it ended about four or five feet below it. Now, certainly, this would be extremely difficult for most adults to climb, but children would have practically no trouble pulling it off. Assuming I was wearing proper shoes, I could have climbed it as well.

I told my students that I thought about the altar as the place where I would soon belong. I told my students about how I thought of the life events that brought me so close to priesthood against all odds. I told my students of how hard I prayed in that chapel... but I also told them about how I thought about what would happen if I tried to climb that fence and prank the nuns. That was foolish of me as a teacher, because all learning in that classroom ceased as soon as that idea left my mouth. All my kids perked up in their chairs, and with what I can only describe as a hive-mind mentality, they strove to unearth any and all information regarding that fence and/or possible nun pranking. I tried to cover my mistake sensibly at first: I told them the truth.

"Kids, please hear me. The answers to all these questions are all the same. If I did anything to those nuns, I would not be ordained a priest and I would be thrown out of seminary in an instant."

That didn't work. They started looking for exceptions to the rule, no matter how crazy. Perhaps it was my second mistake that day, but I tried to forcibly end the conversation.

"Alright, I'm done. From this point on, no more hypothetical questions. So no more questions starting with the words 'what if'. Got it? Alright. Yes, you, what's your question?"

"What if you climbed the..."

"Hey! Didn't you hear what I just said? That's a hypothetical! Next question. Yes, you. What's your question?"

"Suppose that you got into the area by..."

"That's a hypothetical as well. 'Suppose that' is the same things as 'what if'. You, what's your question?"

"Let's say that the nuns are asleep and..."

"Oh, you have got to be kidding me. I'm not answering that! Ugh. Yes, Megan, what's your question?"

"Assuming you got to the top of the fence and came back down the same side before you got caught, would..."

"You're all doing this on purpose! Those questions all end the same way! I get thrown out of seminary! Alright, John, let's hear your question. Don't make me regret this."

"So, in theory, the other side of the fence is still technically the chapel, so wouldn't you be in the same place as before?"

It was about this time that their teacher came to my rescue and firmly closed the discussion. While I was grateful for the bailout, the damage was done. The kids were hopelessly giggly over the prospect of nun pranking, and all I could do was run out the clock and try again the following week.

Then again, perhaps life is simply too amusing to keep such secrets! Perhaps those students needed something silly to laugh at that day? Although I didn't teach them as much as I had originally hoped, I can look back on that day of class and laugh. After all, a joyful day can hardly be considered a wasteful day, in my book.

By contrast, the monastery of Saint John's Abbey in Collegeville was far more down to earth and more about community than isolated prayer. The Abbey is on the campus of Saint John's University, so the isolation of the monastery was enjoyably voluntary. I chose Saint John's Abbey in Collegeville, MN for my annual spiritual retreat after one year of ministry at the parish. I did so for a few sensible reasons: it was far from home but not too far to travel there by car. Family friends were in the area and the abbey came highly recommended by a staff member of mine. Most importantly, it was Benedictine - an order I had little contact with and therefore I had plenty to learn from their way of life.

Although anyone can have a retreat at their location, most people would be directed toward their guest house: a relatively plush set of apartments that was located outside of the monastery itself. However, as an ordained priest on retreat by himself, I was permitted to live within the monastery walls. I was given a vacant room which was ever so slightly better than the ones the monks lived in. I was permitted to walk through the private monastery grounds, I ate and prayed with the monks during normal meal times and prayer times, and I was free to sleep, read, and/or explore as I desired. All-in-all, it was an ideal environment for a spiritual retreat.

It was something of an odd contrast, with respect to Denmark, WI. Instead of cloistered nuns, I had a group of men who were happy to be around me and speak to me - men who welcomed me to join them side-by-side in prayer as well as at table for lunch and dinner. In Denmark, my alone time was profoundly that - time of total isolation. In Collegeville, my alone time was different. I was free to enjoy some quiet in my room or the garden, but I was not entirely alone at any given point: I had an entire community of friendly and compassionate men all around me. At any given moment, I could knock on a door or wander over to the communal lounge - I would almost certainly be greeted by someone willing and able to talk to me about whatever I needed. It was an environment that created a strange sense of peace: I was simultaneously on my own and a part of a community. To state that feeling in an entirely underwhelming manner: it was nice. It was refreshingly nice.

In terms of orthodoxy, I tried to use my time wisely: I had a tablet for my eBooks, but I chose to refrain from using the Wi-Fi for any reason. I knew that I'd slip back into Netflix before long otherwise. I read, I wrote in my journal, I spoke to a priest about the biggest conflicts in my life, and I prayed and attended Mass regularly. The retreat took place almost exactly one year after my ordination, so it was nice to evaluate a year in its entirety. In terms of less-than-orthodox matters, I was pleasantly free to be myself during this week. Spiritual retreats are not times for modern thinking to be beaten out of us. There was never a feeling of being stifled or boxed in by my environment, and I didn't have to pretend I was someone else. Although that might seem like a minor detail, it was a necessary one: without freedom to relax, how could anyone properly reflect upon life? So rather than fearfully reading the Bible in a stone cell by candlelight (a drab stereotype of monastic life), I was able to pursue my mental and emotional wellness in a relaxed and casual manner. As I wandered into the church from time to time for the quiet, I was amused that the church looked like a Klingon Battlecruiser, including the communion rails and stained glass windows. Those silly thoughts come and go, but there was no need to fret over those mini daydreams. When not in prayer, I had the opportunity for an extended tour of the university's pottery department, which is one of the best in the nation. During one of my walks, I noticed that a graduate student of theology was presenting his master's thesis on campus, and it was open to the public: my attendance was enthusiastically appreciated, and I learned a thing or two for my trouble. I also finished the *Harry Potter* series in the monastery garden while smoking a cigar, all of which felt extremely satisfying at the time. The point here is that the entire environment made for an effective spiritual retreat: a time to get away from typical concerns, and a time to rest and reflect upon one's spiritual state. It is not, by contrast, a place to seal yourself from all pleasures and comforts, nor is it a time of voluntary punishment! The ideal place for that kind of rest and reflection is a place that keeps you grounded and reasonable, but also gives you enough personal freedom to be yourself.

Although Saint John's Abbey in Minnesota is not the ideal place for all people, it served me and many others quite well. I do affirm that absolutely everyone has their own place waiting for them and their spiritual retreat. Everyone can benefit from a week without Internet or TV; a week to think and pray about life and one's own state of happiness. It is a worthy use of time and energy, and it does empower you to be better and more focused in the near future. All you need do is make the time and find a place that feels comfortable, yet challenges you to venture out of your comfort zone. Such places may be uncommon, but they are not rare - nor are they particularly difficult to find.

Chapter Seven: The Walls of the Soul's Playground

Now I know that for some of you Americans, this is your first parlay, but there are rules to modern warfare! We're not dumb beasts!

-Commander Livingston, Polite War skit, The Whitest Kids You Know

The title of this chapter will be obvious enough in a few paragraphs. Before that point, however, there is reason to begin with the personal qualities that led me to that phrase in the first place. I am, in one particular way, the opposite of a priestly stereotype: I dread funerals (to a certain extent) and I love weddings (to approximately the same extent). On the one hand, this is a fairly reasonable statement: people naturally want a young priest for their wedding and an old one for their funeral. On the other hand, however, most priests find funerals to be the most meaningful parts of their ministry while I feel exactly the same way about weddings. If you ask a typical parish priest why they favor funerals, they'd say that ordinary people are in a spiritual mood at funerals and there is a far greater chance of them caring about what the church has to offer them. On the other hand, people come to weddings to party, and the priest might as well be a part of the floral arrangements. In my experience, by contrast, funerals are the most awkward of liturgies. People don't know what to do or what to expect. The words of faith and comfort that I have to offer are of use to churchy people and the closest members of the deceased, but I never feel like I have any real ability to reach the people who aren't already on board with the notions of resurrection, or the reality of the human spirit, or the communion of souls. In short, I perpetually feel like I'm only talking to half of the people present. At weddings, I feel better equipped to reach the entire congregation. While preparing for a wedding, I generally assume that 50% of the church will be non-Catholics or Catholics that haven't been in church for quite some time. That assumption, which hopefully isn't accurate for every wedding, is immensely useful. It is good to assume that some people share at least a portion of the church's faith, but it is more reasonable to assume that everyone is coming together to celebrate the marriage of their friend and/or family member. I can work with that! I can work with the notion of people coming together in joy and hope for their loved ones. At a wedding, there can certainly be some Jesus talk thrown in. However, I mainly talk about family, connection, fidelity, and life - those are topics that practically everyone can connect to and/or consider. At a wedding, I can give a message in the language of the people - nearly the entire people, whatever their age or denomination.

For the most part, people are able to enjoy weddings with that theme. The given message is accessible to the people, the ceremony is kept upbeat and jolly, and there isn't any need for wasted time or a drawn out ceremony. In addition to all that, whenever possible, I make the time to attend the reception. At the time of this writing, I have only missed one reception - a necessary decision made with much regret. Not only do I go to the reception, I *celebrate* with everyone else. I talk to new people, I congratulate the couple, I tip the bartenders well, and I let people talk religion/spirituality to me as their needs dictate. Perhaps most importantly, I dance the night away as long as I feel like I'm welcome on the dance floor. When that doesn't happen, I leave the dancers to their fun and call it an early night. When I have a dance partner or two, I stick around for as long as anyone else. Although I do this because I actually do enjoy dancing, I also do it because I want the people to understand that they are worth my time: their wedding is not just an hour or two "at the office" for the priest. For all these reasons, I very often head out to my car with a few people bidding me farewell with the quote "you're the coolest priest ever".

A slight concern over that compliment is the reason for this chapter, really, because I am *not* trying to be a cool priest. I am not trying to pretend that I'm still in my mid-twenties, I am not trying to be the life of the party, and I am not trying to fool people into thinking that I leave my priestly identity at the door when I leave the church for the evening. I am trying to be a good and genuinely spiritual priest while also being myself. Father Justin: the swing dancing priest is not an act or an illusion. That person is me and always is me, even if I don't get much opportunity to break out the dance moves or magic tricks on an ordinary Sunday. Must there be a contradiction between my individual joys and my priestly responsibilities? Both aspects of my personality are real and sacred to me. It would be devastating to be told that I was no longer permitted to dance or play video games. It would also be devastating to be told that I was no longer permitted to celebrate the Mass or hear confessions. Both of those cruel commands would be an absolute attack on my very spirit - an order to somehow be less than my true self. I sincerely hope and pray that such an order never arrives.

With this little nugget of self-understanding firmly in my mind, I read a short but profound statement in the works of G.K. Chesterton. Aside from the fact that I love practically everything that Chesterton wrote, one of his smaller observations struck me in a tremendous way. In the final chapter of his book Orthodoxy, he briefly offered up his brief counter-arguments to what he saw as relatively minor complaints against Catholicism. One such argument was that Catholicism need not be respected or valued because priests were angry old mopes who do nothing but spread misery and guilt to whoever happens to listen to them. To that, Chesterton writes:

"[I regard as a paradox] the view that priests darken and embitter the world. I look at the world and simply discover that they don't. Those countries in Europe which are still influenced by priests, are exactly the countries where there is still singing and dancing and coloured dresses and art in the open-air. Catholic doctrine and discipline may be walls; but they are the walls of a playground."

To that idea, I truly must tip my hat to him. That is, as a matter of fact, the very concept behind the devotions and disciplines of ideal Christian living (which we all, of course, fail to entirely live up to). I have never actually met a priest who was anti-fun: a priest who thought of pleasure or delight as inherently sinful. I have heard of priests before my time who apparently thought that, and upon hearing of such people, my first instinct was to assume some sort of personal struggle or inner turmoil. People do not naturally regard fun as automatically wrong, and there is no real reason for that to change upon ordination to the priesthood. Of course priests want to have fun and enjoy life! They simply have a tendency to have strong opinions as to what sort of fun is healthy and appropriate, and what sort of fun is ultimately harmful or destructive.

Beyond (what I consider to be) the reasonable conclusion that priests are not mopey misery-spreaders, which nevertheless leaves us with the issue of discipline and devotion. For any priest, no matter how fun or wild he may be, must value self-control and tranquility as well. At least, a healthy priest must value those things. How can those two fairly basic facts fit together? Indeed, as Mr. Chesterton asserted decades ago, they fit together like a playground and a surrounding wall. The wall is serious business, as walls often are. Walls are not meant to be played on, aside from the inherent thrill of breaking the rules (which, let's be honest, never goes out of style). That said, walls serve a real and quite clear purpose: they keep harmful things

73

away from vulnerable things. Although we might be annoyed with a wall when it prevents us from going where we want, can you think of a physical wall that has do not serve a worthwhile purpose of some sort? I can call to mind two general examples: the exceptionally rare walls that are purely decoration (often found in gardens), and walls within ruins that are no longer accompanied by the thing they were protecting or the structure they were sustaining. All-in-all, if you encounter a wall in the real world, you can bet that the wall was built for some objective and pragmatic purpose. Walls, generally speaking, are not decorative or superficial structures; they are practical to the extent that we might call their very nature "utilitarian".

Now apply that principle to a system of rules. Ignoring, for a moment, outdated rules that no longer serve their originally intended purpose, rules by-and-large exist to achieve some concrete objective. "Thou shalt not steal" is clearly a rule that protects everyone's property. Speed limits exist to make the roads safer and more orderly. "Don't give hungry people scorpions" became a rule because of Jesus' compassion for all living things, including poisonous arachnids*. Rules are rarely fun to observe, as we all know. I rarely drive slower than ten miles over the speed limit. I also occasionally steal combs from funeral homes. And once I gave a scorpion sucker to a hungry person. Hopefully my minor confessions prove my point: rules can be tough to follow! That does *not* make them worthless - in fact, you can count on the worthwhile things in life to be difficult in some way or another!

*Jesus may have been concerned about people getting poisoned by the scorpions, I suppose. But I choose to believe that Jesus specifically had a love for one of the most reviled life forms that crawl upon the earth. Call me an idealist if you must.

I don't believe in rules that serve no purpose. My mother had a few rules about breakfast that made no sense. At the top of the list: no chocolate cereal for breakfast. Heresy! That sort of sheer matriarchal dominance of the breakfast table ruled our kitchen for the first sixteen years of my life. For that entire period, I tried and failed to comprehend my mother's labyrinthine system of what was or was not "proper" breakfast food. By way of example, chocolate cereal may have been literally packaged by the devil - so strong was the evil that my mother detected in the breakfast isle of the grocery store. Yet oddly enough, chocolate donuts were acceptable, as were chocolate chip pancakes. I consider it fortunate that I was not driven mad by the experience. Luckily, relief came my way at age sixteen in the form of a driver's license. Amen amen, I say to you: the first thing I did with that thing was to drive the car to Sentry foods and purchase a box of chocolate cereal. The next morning was... unique, to say the least. I came downstairs to witness my brother and father chomping down on chocolate cereal, with my mother looking on in absolute rage and horror. That morning, she took my license away from me on the grounds that I had abused the privilege. Later that afternoon, my dad gave it back to me with a grin on his face. "Nice work, Justin, I'm proud of you." I still remember those words like it was yesterday: my first rebellious victory against silly and pointless rules. There would be others down the road.

Getting back to the matter at hand, I can respect rules that serve a purpose - and I can respect them, even if I struggle to obey them. Are there pointless and/or outdated rules in Catholicism? Probably. A fair amount of ancient Rome lives on in the Church, and old habits die hard: bad habits doubly so. Still, chances are good that the number of pointless or outdated rules is far lower than most people would assume. With a proper focus on Canon Law (AKA church law) as a whole, the rules that govern the faith are remarkably pragmatic. I assert an unpopular opinion: the rules of Catholicism can all be reasonably explained with the overall

goodness and prosperity of humanity (remember the playground from the analogy above?) as its

ultimate goal. You may very well disagree with that explanation. However, upon a moderate

degree of examination, I have come to discover that the rules are not arbitrary or senseless. They

are tiny parts of vast wall, and taken together, they encircle something inspiring and wonderful…

but tragically fragile.

Chapter Eight: The Vitality of Good Company

River of God, there's an eclipse of the sun,
The darkness is rising, we're all on the run.

Forgive us our failings,
Forgive us our wailings,

When love is not love,
Then the darkness will come.

And when love is within,
All the light will return.

Like a river of love,
Like a river of sun.
-"River of God", by Linda Perhacs, *The Soul of All Natural Things*

This might be the most obvious and common-sense chapter. Everyone knows that good

company is good and bad company is bad. Even the most devoted relativist would agree it's

probably wise to stay away from people who depress or upset you. The purpose here is not to prove the point: the point is far too obvious and clear for that. Rather, here is what good company looks like and why bad company is best avoided.

Now, first and foremost, you can tell what good company is by a few key indications. In the context of my specific life and relationships, the top five qualities of good company involves people who:

1. Laugh often, and laugh with you.

2. Are capable of hard work, at least when necessary.

3. Inspire you to do better, whether through positive feedback or respectful criticism.

4. Will teach you something, but also be willing to learn from you.

5. Can temper honesty with care.

Good company will somehow bring out the best in you, with no need for shaming, manipulation, or abuse. Shaming, manipulation, and abuse are perhaps the worst daily enemies to an ordinary sense of happiness in life, and the worst thing about it is that we let them into our lives. We allow ourselves to be mistreated, over a long period of time. Good company does not do that. Or at the very least, good company rarely does that but is willing to learn from mistakes and guarantee that such hurt is not repeated in the future. After all, good people mess up from time to time. Some degree of forgiveness and leniency are a part of the process.

Now make no mistake: I adore my friends now that I'm an adult. I adore my friends now that I know the difference between a good friend and a bad one. Anyone whom I call a friend today can safely apply to our relationship at least four out of five of my above "good company" conditions. In these last two years, I have not experienced a great deal of friendship - ministry just took up too much of my time and my friends were relatively far away. But when I think of good friends and good company, I think of specific people without hesitation. I know that there are people in my life who add to my life, rather than take away from it. Of course, they all do so in unique ways. In fact, when I think of the people of my life as a whole, one specific person personifies each of one of my top five qualities for good company. Those five people encapsulate the values of laugher, hard work, inspiration, two-way education, and caring honesty.

Laughing good company: Lex Cashore

The laughing friend of my life is, without doubt, my best friend Lex. We are constantly celebrating the ridiculousness of life itself. Between the tendency to put googly eyes on practically everything (from my shirt to my driver's license to baked fish) and Lex's willingness to give amusing commentary on life or media, there is never a time that we don't laugh with each other for at least a little while. Also, Lex loves to be around other people while I somehow make a fool of myself. Once the key phrase of silliness has been said, Lex will lean to the nearest person and whisper in their ear, "That guy's a Catholic priest." If the fortunate (unfortunate?) stranger inquires about that, Lex will go on to explain that literally everything is funnier when done by a Catholic priest. Notable examples include, but are not limited to: a beard of bees, French trash talk, muttonchops, an adverse hatred for chickens, and the severe pummelings by five-year-olds. Yes, I know I should win those fights more often.

Lex and I don't currently live in the same city, so we see each other every other month at best. I dearly wish we were closer during day-to-day life, because when something unusual or unique happens to me or around me, I want someone to share that moment with. If that aforementioned unique moment of life is something to be laughed at and enjoyed, it will probably be even more enjoyable with someone at your side with a compatible sense of humor.

Lex and I are at our best in such circumstances: riding the waves of unpredictability and absurdity. In 2005, when we both lived in Madison, we once overheard a strange comment which may or may not have been a joke:

"Real men wear pinstripes."

Real men wear pinstripes? It was an odd and unexpected thing to hear. At first, we didn't react in any special way. We embraced the joke and expanded it a bit. At least for the two of us, there are only a few ways to truly prove one's manliness: men drink martinis, resolve disagreements through arm wrestling, ride on horseback whenever possible, or wear pinstripe clothing. No exceptions. So if you claim to be a man, but you're sober, wearing jeans, and not arm wrestling someone, you better be on horseback. The definition of manhood remains uncontested to this day, as far as Lex and I are concerned.

Of course, that somewhat shallow inside joke is not terribly special when taken on its own. Everyone jokes around with friends at some point. However, Lex and I weren't done. Lex had managed to sufficiently illustrate my lack of masculinity to the point where I went to a men's formal clothing shop, Jazzman on State St, and bought a pair of gray 1960's style pinstripe pants. After all, I'm terrible at arm wrestling, I can't drinking alcohol in any competitive sense of the word, and I don't own a horse.

Lex was delighted at that decision. A more sensible person than I would have used their scraps of disposable income for food, gas, or books. Instead, I bought an expensive pair of pants that I couldn't use for anything other than wedding apparel or swing dances. So naturally, we had to celebrate my exceptional sense of fiscal responsibility. That evening went down in history as "Manhood Day". Although we both worked weekends, we managed to find a Friday night where we free at the same time. I was the night auditor of a hotel, which is the employee who tends to the front desk during the night and does basic accounting and bookkeeping during the quiet hours of the night. So we had time between the end of Lex's shift at 7:00 PM and the start to my graveyard shift at 10:00 PM. I headed off to Lex's place where we both got ready for the evening: we both had pinstripe clothing on, and we got some artificial facial hair for good measure – a dandy handlebar mustache for myself, and Lex took the muttonchops.

From there, we headed off to some bar to drink and play pool. The facts that Lex doesn't really drink and both of us are terrible pool players were completely irrelevant. We happened to have a great time. We actually did play a proper game of pool at a college sports bar in downtown Madison, Lex spilled someone's glass on accident – providing the opportunity for Lex to buy someone a drink, and we took a few pictures along the way. Of course, we only spoke in terrible British accents throughout the entire evening (as befitting our facial hair), and absolutely refused to shy away from anyone who found our behavior to be a bit odd. In fact, Lex absolutely thrives on such attention. Lex must have had the same conversation three times over, with different people who were bold enough to approach us:

"Hi, you two know that you look really out place here, right?"

"Yes, we know. This isn't really our usual thing, but today is special."

"Oh? What's so special about today?"

"We're celebrating the fact that Justin is now a real man!" At that line, the bar patron got more serious and tried to find something appropriate with which to respond.

"Oh! Well, that certainly is a big deal. Congrats to him, I suppose."

"He appreciates it. He had to save up a while to afford it."

"Oh! I can only imagine how much it all must have been!"

"About eighty bucks. That's how much those pants cost. Now that he owns pinstripe pants, he's a real man." This was generally the point where the other person would put realize that the two of them were talking about two separate things.

"Uh, ok. Well, have a good night, I guess." Of course, all that was within earshot of me, so we were able to savor the double entendre together after the conversation concluded.

That whole night was a fun one, and certainly a major highlight of that year. With the inside joke of "Manhood Day" surviving as long as it did, Lex and I decided to do it again last year; we dubbed it "Manhood Day's ten-year anniversary". I drove to Madison, joined Lex and few other friends in the area, and we headed down to a bar for beer and arm wrestling. As a bonus, they also had a classic arcade hockey game – the one that plays like foosball, with spin-able poles that control one or two hockey players at a time. We figured hockey was manly enough for a game or two.

Perhaps the most relevant Lex-related factor is this: Lex and I don't have that much in common. While we certainly have a common appreciation for certain hobbies on general principle, our specific preferences are substantially less related. However, all of our differences and disagreements completely and totally pale in comparison to our shared love for life in all its bizarre and unpredictable glory. I have faith that Lex and I will be laughing side-by-side until our very lungs give out, and life without Lex is one of the few things I cannot bear to imagine. Good company.

Hard working good company: Lawrence Lopina

The hard working person of my life is a tricky one to nail down; there are, after all, several people worthy of title. However, in the end, it's got to go to my dad. Is that answer at least partially unfair? Totally. Whether we see them as good or bad, the way we see our fathers is as biased and skewed as anything can be. Yet I make my assertion all the same. While I certainly laugh often with my dad, and while he's certainly good for a life lesson here and there (normally over brandy Manhattans), my dad is good company because of his work ethic. It is also important to note that his work ethic does not simply exist for eight hours a day, nor is it dependent whatsoever on earning that week's paycheck. His work ethic is firmly rooted in his bones, and it applies to his work and leisure alike.

Now, to be fair, a truly hardworking dad is not always a good thing. During the years we lived on the lake, while I was in high school, my dad somehow came up with a different project by the week. "Hey Eric and Justin! We've got a whole Saturday open and the weather is perfect. Let's tear up the dock, realign the support struts, and put the dock back together again better than ever!"

That horrible day was the worst of all, literally spent waist-deep in mud and grime, while doing repairs that none of us were qualified to do in the first place. For the record, the dock was not improved by our repairs - not even using the broadest use of the word "repairs".

My dad would also work a little too hard in matters that most people would consider petty or at least unworthy of the effort. At that same house, a muskrat was wreaking havoc in our backyard. For an "animals are great as long as I don't have to feed them or clean up after them" person such as myself, a local muskrat is just a fact of life to be accepted. I couldn't care less that one was living in the vicinity. For my father, a local muskrat was a cause for war upon nature itself. I feel comfortable describing it that way, because the yard looked like a battlefield in the end. My dad and my brother dug so many holes to root out the animal, it would be difficult for a passerby to tell their efforts apart from a light artillery shelling. To this day, whenever I see an R.U.O.S. (Rodent Of Unusual Size), I immediately picture my dad flipping out and pummeling it to death with his bare fists.

The muskrat story is just one reason of many for why I love him. However, it doesn't quite address the reason he's good company: he will never take the easy way out if it means that others pay the price. My dad will see that something is done right and done well, whenever possible. If you need help, Larry Lopina is someone you can rely upon. He doesn't make excuses when it's his turn to do the dishes after dinner; he won't turn away someone in need of some financial advice (he's an accountant by trade); and he's reasonably punctual for a Lopina.

In my mind, there was one event that elevated him from "normal hard working man" to "saintly father figure for all". If it were ever my call, I'd make him Larry the Fiscally Responsible, Patron Saint of Business Ethics. You see, for the bulk of my life, my father was the Vice President and part owner of a medium-sized printing company. That company served him well (and vice versa) and that job was able to afford him a good life with enough money to help put three biological children through college and adopt a daughter from China. At the time of this writing, my sister has a few years to go before college, so we'll see about whether or not my dad contributes to her higher education like his three other children. Odds are pretty good, though. My father held the same job for many years and took his responsibilities seriously, so life was pretty sweet until the late '90s or so. The company took a huge risk and bought a massive and expensive printer, ideal for the company's primary focus of printed high-quality color advertisement materials. Long story short, it was a good idea as long as they had the business to keep it operating. If the work slacked off, they wouldn't be able to pay it off and would ultimately prove more of a liability than an asset. As luck and/or fate would have it, the economy tanked a couple of years later and the printed advertisement business was hit hard during the resulting recession. The company had to fight tooth and nail, simply to hold onto its longest and most loyal customers. It was bad, and without some kind of miracle, the writing was, as they say, on the wall.

The sad part of this story is that the precise miracle we were all hoping for did not come. The economy did not recover, and the company's fate descended into all-but-certain doom. Of course, my father continued to work his fingers to the bone. There were daily needs to be met, regardless of future occurrences, and my father made it his mission to close the company in a dignified and responsible way. After years of poor business, the company had accumulated quite a bit of debt; were the company to close overnight without warning, disaster would certainly result. This was my father's reoccurring nightmare and worst-case-scenario: running out of time and declaring bankruptcy. If that was to happen, the business's various creditors would never receive the money they were owed - businesses that had a right to that money and deserved to have their business deals honored. The owners of the company, my father included, might have been sued by the bank as well as the printer's union: which means my family would lose every dime we'd saved, regardless of our independence to the business's financial difficulties.

Eventually, my dad found the way out. After failed attempt after failed attempt, the business was sold to another mid-level company of similar specialization. So in the end, all creditors got their money. All significant equipment went to good use, as many people as possible got to keep their jobs, and everyone who had to move on received ample time to find new employment as well as just severance pay. When the doors finally closed, I was under the impression that everyone who wanted a new job was able to find one. No one was sued, and the closing of the company was worth approximately two seconds of airtime on the local news. Dad found that the company deserved far more respect than that after decades of good and faithful business, and I can't fault him for thinking that way.

Currently, my dad is doing similar financial work a few miles from his old place. He isn't making quite as much as before, and is still working more hours than I feel he deserves. While the reduced income bothers some of the family, I wish my father would have more time away from work now that he's in his mid-50's with a punk teenage daughter to look after. As his child most unconcerned with money, perhaps my opinion isn't all that convincing. I make it all the same: he made it through the years where people were counting on his income level; he made it through the years where an 80-hour workweek was at least occasionally the moral choice. I want my dad to be happy and around the people who truly care about him. It's a matter of principle, really. My dad has proven himself when it mattered the most. He faithfully provided for his family and his employees for years. He was there when he was needed the most. He will forever be, at least to me, the Patron Saint of Business Ethics. The model of a hard worker. Good company.

One quick footnote: my dad is also really funny. Unless you're my mom. In that case, he's goofy and annoyingly sarcastic. For the rest of us, though, that just makes him more funny.

Inspirational good company: Heather Hruby

Out of the list of the many people who have inspired me to do better, the one who somehow stands out is my good friend Heather. Although inspiration can come from anywhere, Heather is a clear case of how inspiration can work through the simple power of the spoken word.

Heather and I spent a great deal of time together in high school (1996-2000) and we kept in frequent contact during our college years. Soon after that, she got married and moved to Iowa, which made face-to-face times a bit difficult to manage. Still, I consider it something of a personal code of honor to visit the family in Iowa once a year - although I sadly no longer have a 100% success record. To this day, Heather remains one of the greatest and kindest people on the planet, and she remains proof enough for me that goodness and gentleness not only exist in this world but exist in a sustainable and lasting way. That is to say, people occasionally try to talk to me about peace as merely time between wars: the "ideal life" we read about in story books is mere fantasy 98% of the time. These people would say that when life is good, that is the cosmos giving you a little coffee break before the next catastrophe hits you. When those sorts of things are spoken in my presence, I think of Heather and I immediately feel better. While I'm sure her life isn't "perfect", she is living proof that grace does, in fact, belong in this world and will thrive when given the chance.

Why do I think so high and lofty of this high school friend, even fifteen years after those schoolyears have come and gone? Certainly there are many reasons, some less mature than others. However, there is one concrete reason. Heather was inspirational enough to jostle me out of teenage angst-style stupidity at the height of its power over me. Around 1998 or 1999, Heather and I had our drivers' licenses, and the two of us would visit one another's house with some frequency. Her family liked me and my family adored her, so it was never much of an issue. Well, one day Heather came by the house on a Saturday fairly late in the evening by high schooler standards. If I had to guess, she arrived around 8:00 or 9:00 pm. At least at the Lopina household back then, 9:00 pm was the time when friends ought to be leaving, not arriving. But Heather was an angel among mere mortals, so my parents let it slide. After a little while, my parents began getting ready for bed on the second floor of the house. Heather and I remained in the TV room downstairs near the garage door - it was like a living room, but more for the kids than the adults. The adults tended to prefer the great room on the same floor as my parent's bedroom - it had a better TV, the grand piano, and the bar. Now that I'm 34, I'd certainly take the great room for absolutely any social gathering.

The reason I'm setting the scene is this: Heather and I were alone, late at night, in a comfortable room, far from the prying eyes of my parents. How did we spend the time, dare you ask? We spent the whole night sitting next to each other on the couch... debating moral philosophy. No, that's not a joke nor an exaggeration. For hours, we ceaselessly discussed and considered the notion of goodness in the span of a human life. How does one live the best that they can? Where does happiness and satisfaction and fulfillment lie? It wasn't an easy talk, nor a short one. But it was interesting. I loved every minute of it.

For the most part, we spent the majority of our time arguing the opposite points of one major philosophical idea. Consistent with my frustrations in life at the time, I took the stance of the grumpy teenage boy. I asserted the fact that to get the most out of life, one must focus on one's own wants, needs, and desires. Service, especially unpaid service, must be seen as a temporary distraction or delay on the road to fulfillment. I never believed service was a bad thing, I merely had begun to see it as something that was not truly a part of a genuine life journey. Now that my vocabulary is more developed, I was advocating a philosophy of hedonism - although even in my most selfish state, my idea of hedonism was far from mere physical pleasures and instant gratification. Rather, Justin Lopina-style hedonism was an egocentric worldview that focused on personal goals and desires, be they proficiency in a musical instrument or the freedom to spend your time as you like. The needs of others simply wasn't a part of the picture. Thank God I grew out of that! I am quite certain that such a version of me would have grown up to be truly lonesome, and therefore profoundly miserable.

Heather, the more Jesus-like of the two of us, essentially argued the exact opposite idea: that service to God and neighbor was, in fact, the only true path to peace, contentment, and lasting joy. One could live one's own life and care for one's neighbor as oneself, at the same time.

We argued and talked long into the night, with Heather finally heading home well after midnight. My memory tells me that she left home around 4:00 am... I'm sure in reality it was closer to 1 am or 2 am. Nevertheless, I had a profoundly amusing and awkward talk waiting for me the next morning. My parents were fully prepared to ambush me the second I came up to the kitchen for breakfast. The ambush was a joint effort on their part, and with so much time that has passed, I cannot even remember which one was specifically doing the talking. In my memory, I picture them both asking the same questions at the same time: parenting in stereo.

"Justin, is there anything you feel the need to tell us?"

"Uh, no. Not really."

"About last night?"

"Oh, did we make too much noise? Sorry about that, I thought we kept our voices down pretty well."

"No, Justin, your volume was fine. We know Heather was here for quite a while."

"Yes, she was. We didn't plan to stay up that late, but we were having a very interesting discussion."

"So what were the two of you really doing?"

"We really were just talking. Most of it was moral philosophy, actually."

89

"Justin! You were alone, downstairs, with Heather, for hours on end in the middle of the night. Seriously, what were the two of you doing? Just be honest with us!"

"I'm being dead serious! We were debating moral philosophy! That was it, really!"

I shudder a little bit when I think back on that conversation, because I continue to be amazed that my parents didn't interrogate me longer than they did. In life, we all have many moments where we unsuccessfully attempt to communicate a truth that is too outlandish for people be believe outright. Notable examples might include "I've changed this time, it will never happen again", "that was not just a dream, it was real", and "seriously, it's not what it looks like - the bathroom sink sprayed all this water on my pants". However, all those statements put together would still be an easier undertaking than explaining to parents that their seventeen-year-old son spent an entire evening alone with their closest female friend... to talk about morality. No parent will ever believe that.

Here's the reason I'm putting Heather in the "inspirational" category instead of the "instructional" category: I don't remember a single detail with respect to her argument that night. I remember her overall point, stated above, and nothing else. That's probably normal, given how much time has passed. However, even if the logic and the concrete ideas have faded into distant memory, I still remember the effect it all had on my very soul. In all seriousness, I started thinking differently after that night - she permanently changed my thought pattern. I also felt different about things as well - so my mind and my heart were influenced together. That's what makes it inspirational: it was life-changing.

With Heather, more than knowledge was as at work: it was knowledge and wisdom. Heather sees the world in a very Christ-like way, and she always has. And that night, she managed to somehow gift me with a small portion of that sight. It remains with me today, and I know that I would have been a very different person without her in those early and formative years. Good company.

Teaching and learning good company: Rick Kempf

Another friend of mine serves as a fine example for quality #4: the ability to teach as well as be taught. Frankly, it's the combination that's the true challenge. Most people are either capable of learning, or instructing in some way. It's the person who is able to do both that excels in the lives of others. My friend Rick has displayed that dual quality, at least in my presence, in last couple of years. Rick and I met through common friends, and our key interests were the same - capoeira and gaming, mostly - and we were both happy to spend time at a Madison teashop with everyone else. Capoeira is a Brazilian martial art that depends upon rhythm and gymnastic motion. While it has a strong following in South America, there are mere pockets of interest here in the Midwest. Therefore, Rick and I were automatically part of a small group of people; it did not take terribly long for us to meet and realize that we shared a common group of friends and acquaintances.

Well, when a group of friends talks for a reasonable length of time, controversial topics will inevitably come up. With an off-duty priest in group, you can go right ahead and cut that "reasonable length of time" in half. So, about at the time when our friendship was going from "friends of friends" to "people who actually enjoy each others' occasional company", Rick enjoyed my presence but was somewhat bothered by the fact that I was a practicing Catholic. So one evening, with just a touch of confrontation in his voice, asked me point-blank, "Justin, do you believe in evolution?"

It was an easy question, and I answered "yes" without any hesitation in my voice. As soon as I spoke, I could tell that I threw him off a bit. It seemed as though he was expecting the other answer, and had some follow up statements prepared for that eventuality. Much to my relief, however, my answer eased a great deal of tension. You see, Rick differentiated himself from many others that day by his willingness to let go of the stereotypes that stick to Christians (especially Catholics). There are few things as frustrating to me these days as someone who is angry at the church for some reason (usually a valid reason, more or less), and who will not be calmed down or reasoned with. Some people call such encounters "brick wall talks". We've all had those, we've all been the brick wall at some point, as well. However, brick wall talks are monumentally disheartening when you genuinely want to help the person you're talking to, to acknowledge their pain, and assert some level of two-way friendship or respect. When the anger/stubbornness/hatred is just too much for that to happen, those two people will have a great deal of difficulty restoring whatever level of communication they had before. It was nice to know that Rick was not the sort of person to easily fall into such mentality. He could be reasoned with. He was willing to learn from someone else.

For roughly four years, Rick and I saw one another here and there during my visits to Madison. Within those four years, Rick and I both had our share of problems. Although they weren't identical problems, we were able to empathize with one another fairly easily. Around the end of my seminary training, with my priestly ordination looming in just a few short months, we randomly had a large chunk of time to ourselves. That particular night, Rick planned a grilled cheese potluck at his place, where a number of my other friends lived with him as roommates. It seemed like a great opportunity to see the whole group, in addition to enjoying Rick's cooking. I got into Madison, dropped by the apartment in plenty of time, and Rick prepped the frying pans.

92

He had at least six variations of grilled cheese to experiment with, between the various breads, cheeses, and other ingredients. Before the actual cooking began, the kitchen's countertop was an impressive sight.

Sadly, the potluck never got off the ground in spite of its promising beginnings. Between a capoeira event and a show downtown, most of our friends were unable to drop by for any length of time. Not even the temptation of free food was enough. So although Rick and I weren't alone for the entire evening, we had two hour-long periods of time with no other people around to distract us. We spent the first hour making sample-sized grilled cheeses, and comparing the cheese and bread combos. The lack of other people wasn't all that bad: we got to guiltlessly eat all the samples ourselves! By the time the second hour rolled around, we were no longer especially hungry and we were losing hope that anyone else would show up for the potluck. So we grabbed our drinks and sat down on the couch to comfortably talk about how crazy life had been for the two of us during the last few years.

It proved to be a powerful hour, for us both. He was the only person in my life that year that made me feel better (and hopeful for the future) with respect to a difficult and stressful individual in my life at that time. His advice and observations were borne from his personal struggles, so they had the authority of real life behind them. Of course, he also wanted to genuinely help me the best way that he could, and that carries its own sort of authority. Now, although the exact nature of that conversation must remain confidential (therefore, Rick's portion of this chapter is a bit smaller than the other four), the overall effect was that Rick challenged me to think about an old assumption in a new way. He had been willing to do that for me four years ago, and if for no other reason, it was right and just to return the favor. He had proven what sort of guy he was when it counted. Good company.

Honest & caring good company: Father Charles Brown

Finally, there are people who manage to temper honesty with care, no easy thing. First of all, the world is full of brutally honest people. It is true that brutal honesty is better than dishonesty, but such candor can often be so painful to the receiver that the truth does more harm than good in the long run. Likewise, there are people like me who care deeply about others... and let their care occasionally serve as an excuse to stay quiet instead of saying something unpleasant but necessary. Honesty and empathy are, ironically, a difficult combo to manage.

The person this calls to mind is my favorite Scripture professor, Father Brown. Father Brown was a teacher with a mixed reputation, as of 2013. Many people disliked his attitude, found his humor a bit too strange, or were bothered by the lessons he emphasized. As it happens, he was the ideal teacher for me: his attitude wasn't smug, it was merely his confidence. I liked his humor, and for the most part, we saw eye-to-eye on the most vital aspects of the faith. One of his opening remarks for his classes was his own declaration of faith. He began by explaining:

"Class, this is where you are going to learn about why the Bible is the way it is, the literary devices and extra-Biblical influences that shaped so many of our sacred stories - be they Babylonian creation myths leading to Genesis, or the Greek mystery cults as a precursor to Christ's death and resurrection. It is my job to teach you that. But I want you all to know that I absolutely believe in the Incarnation and Resurrection of Christ. If I did not believe that, I would not be a priest. In that case, I'd become a Hindu: their religion has more color!" At that point, I knew that I could trust him as a teacher. He promised the entire class that he would not sugar-coat the truth for the sake of religious scrupulosity, and he promised that such a thing can be

94

done with one's faith remaining intact. In truth, it's moments like that that vitalize my confidence in the Catholic priesthood.

In any event, classes with Father Brown got off to a good start, and I did well for one whole class and the first half of another before I encountered the biggest challenge of my Scriptural education. I learned that the story of the Transfiguration is not likely to be a historical moment of Christ's earthly ministry, while studying contemporary and mainstream Catholic Scripture commentary. I was surprised to read this and a bit shocked, because the Transfiguration is one of my favorite moments in Christ's life to meditate upon. I had always prided myself on my willingness to learn hard truths about the Bible, and my honest tendency to think differently than what we call "fundamentalism" today. This time, however, I found those values hard to live up to. Naturally, I went to Father Brown for help and to set me straight. The meeting didn't go the way I thought it would. Father Brown humbled me with a two-pronged attack. First, he walked me through the development of the Transfiguration as a post-Ascension story that was placed earlier in the Gospels as a way of foreshadowing. Put bluntly, the Transfiguration is a literary device meant to prepare the reader for the radicalness of the Resurrection and Ascension. It wasn't what I wanted to hear, but I knew I had to take this lesson to heart. His attack on my overconfidence came next, as he explained the importance of understanding the Gospel writers, what they were trying to accomplish and communicate, and who they were trying to communicate it to. At first, I was insulted that he had to say those things out loud, as I have indeed tried to keep those considerations at the forefront of my mind...

Yet, for all the unexpected pain and shock, I needed to work through that process at least once during my studies. After all, don't we all need an occasional reminder with respect to how little we know and how far we still have to go? If that is indeed a reasonable stance to take, then

95

I'm glad my big one with Father Brown. He was able to knock that bit of sense into me without too much lasting damage to my self-confidence, or the way I view Scripture overall. Many people are not so lucky.

I came to view Father Brown's talk in light of a Gospel story that is often quoted about others, but rarely quoted about oneself. It's the story of the Rich Young Man.

Now someone approached him and said, "Teacher, what good must I do to gain eternal life?" He answered him, "Why do you ask me about the good? There is only One who is good. If you wish to enter into life, keep the commandments." He asked him, "Which ones?" And Jesus replied, "'You shall not kill; you shall not commit adultery; you shall not steal; you shall not bear false witness; honor your father and your mother'; and 'you shall love you neighbor as yourself.'" The young man said to him, "All of these I have observed. What do I still lack?" Jesus said to him, "If you wish to be perfect, go, sell what you have and give to [the] poor, and you will have treasure in heaven. Then come, follow me." Matt 19:16-22, Catholic Study Bible, 2nd Edition. New American Bible translation.

That story is often used to shame someone into humility: "you need to let go of your possessions", or "you need to remember how much of a sinner you really are", or some other phrase amounting to "don't be like the rich young man." However, we rarely empathize with what that rich young man must have been feeling by the end of that story. Harsh lessons come with a degree of despair, and the rich young man can be pitied just as easily as he can be judged and shamed. Then again, perhaps it is not easy to pity him... perhaps you have to have a "Rich

Young Man" moment first. That "Rich Young Man moment" is indeed how I remember that afternoon in Father Brown's office. It even has its own title in my memory: The Story of the Rich Young Seminarian. I was a version of the rich young man from the Bible, and Father Brown was like Jesus Christ with male-pattern baldness and a preference for corduroy jackets.

"Oh Father Brown, what must I do to inherit Sacred Scripture?"

"My son, you must love the Bible with your whole heart, your whole mind, and your whole soul."

"Yeah, I got that! Totally! What else can I do? Come on, tell me, I'm ready!"

"Well then, my son, you must understand that the Bible contains divine and human truths and we must examine our sacred stories in light of historical contexts, literary traditions, and even the personal agendas of the individual writers."

"Yeah, I got all that! Totally! I'm right there with you, amen! What else can I do?"

"Well then, my son, you must let go of the Transfiguration as you currently understand it." And indeed the rich young seminarian went away sad, for he had much love for the Transfiguration.

Difficult lessons require good teachers; anyone can teach the easy stuff. If someone in your life can guide you through the challenging truths you're likely to ignore on your own, that alone makes them good company.

It should be noted that my top five list of important qualities of good company is hardly exhaustive. Whether you would wish to add a couple of new ones onto my list, or start from scratch, the point is essentially the same. Good people add to your life, and your memories of those people tend to last. My five qualities are derived from some of the most positive memories I draw strength from. If you think back to the warmest memories of your life, shared with the best people you had at the time, what patterns can you discern? Humor? Humility? Kindness?

Selflessness?

Are those same qualities, at least in some way, a part of you? How might you be remembered in the minds of your loved ones?

Chapter Nine: Spiritual Warfare

The Lord has delivered his people, the remnant of Israel. Behold, I will bring them back from the land of the north; I will gather them from the ends of the world, with the blind and the lame in their midst, the mothers and those with child; they shall return as an immense throng. They departed in tears, but I will lead them to brooks of water, on a level road, so that none shall stumble. For I am a father to Israel, Ephraim is my first born. Then the virgins shall make merry and dance, and young men and old as well. I will turn their mourning into joy, I will console and gladden them after their sorrows. –Jeremiah 31: 7b-9; 13, The New American Bible. New American Bible translation.

Spiritual warfare is a term that can certainly be abused by excessive frequency. It can be a way for people to show resentment toward some unknown frustration in their life, like someone who remains unable to find gainful employment. It might be said by parents, when their kids stop coming to church in spite of their upbringing. Spiritual warfare could also be the way someone describes an ongoing conflict that is not the product of one single person. In other words, the words "spiritual warfare" can be used as a sort of spiritual scapegoat: without someone or something concrete to blame, the devil is an ever-present standby.

However, I also assert that spiritual warfare can be a real thing. I also believe it's more prevalent than we give it credit for. It seems to be something that impacts everyone for at least a little while in life; and for some people, it is a constant struggle in life with no real end in sight. However, as Jeremiah proclaimed so long ago, the faithful remnant will one day find relief from the struggles that shall seem like an entire lifetime's worth of suffering. That can be a difficult message to put your faith in, when you're fully immersed in that very same suffering. Then again, that makes the message all the more vital to hear – such times are when messages of hope are needed the most.

What is spiritual warfare, in a nutshell? What is it besides an abstract blame-game? Spiritual warfare is that perpetual struggle (that we all participate in) to make the world a better place. The truth resides in the generality of that statement. Spiritual warfare is not one specific thing; it is a collective struggle of values. On one side, the ultimately victorious side, is wisdom, freedom, truth, justice, mercy, dignity, joy, creativity, and peace. On the other side, the side that must fail by its very nature, you will surely find selfishness, cruelty, murder, theft, oppression, deception, pain, hopelessness, and all forms of slavery. This means that all people who live in the spirit of Christ engage in spiritual warfare on many different kinds of battlefronts.

-The boss who fights to provide their employees with fair wages and benefits, even as his superiors are urging cutbacks, is certainly engaging in spiritual warfare. In fact, that warfare is only intensified if those same employees are unaware of their boss' struggle on their behalf.

-The teacher who refuses to let harm come to their students is certainly experiencing spiritual warfare when their colleagues refuse to see a dangerous influence within the school.

-A child who fights to keep their own hope alive in the face of unrelenting bullies in school is fighting a quiet spiritual warfare, and any success they earn will initially benefit no one but themselves. Still, it remains a battleground like any other, because the world will certainly be a darker place if their self-esteem is entirely crushed by those bullies. On the other hand, a spiritual victory may provide that child with the strength and experience to help others later in life.

-A scientist, with no real sense of faith (pardon the stereotype), attempts to illustrate an important objective truth to the public. When their series of empirical facts requires a sacrifice or lifestyle change from the very public it's intended for, the scientist suffers tremendous backlash from the media as well as from their financial backers. The spiritual warfare begins when that scientist refuses to abandon or recant their findings. Even without an explicit expression of faith, that scientist and seeker of truth begins to fight on Christ's side when they make the choice that authentic truth is more important than personal convenience.

-A person of any demographic knows spiritual warfare when they offer a sympathetic ear to a friend and listens to their hurt and pain. To be a source of encouragement and personal dignity is enough to enlist someone against whatever forces gather in to make human beings less than they are. If you believe that people are more than resources to be harvested, and if you believe that the world is more than a pile of gold to be divided among its rulers, then you have had at least a taste of spiritual warfare. Whether the stakes are an entire city or one lonely stranger, have faith that there is something genuine to gain. To be victorious in spiritual warfare, one need not become a priest or formally work in the public sector. A healthy sense of what is right (and what is wrong) is enough for anyone to be an asset to God and humanity, provided that it comes with the determination to act upon that sense of what is right and just.

So in a way, this is a cold war, with spies aplenty for both sides. Anyone you see on the street may be struggling and fighting for their very life... and waiting in line for their mocha latte. This is a kind of conflict that transcends: borders of faith, nationality, sexuality, and income level. There is absolutely no free thinking person on earth who is exempt from moral responsibility. The only people exempt from that innate duty to do what is right and just are those individuals in comas, those suffering from a mental illness that impairs their ability to know (right from wrong), or those with a complete inability to control their actions. Perhaps there is a simpler way to state that: to know the difference between right and wrong is to possess the responsibility to act upon that very knowledge.

With the outline of the war laid out, the next step is illustrate a typical example of the enemy. Of course, the important enemy to identify is the one most likely to be encountered. Obviously, there are true "bad guys" in the world today. Terrorists, murderers, human traffickers, and sex abusers require no space here. The evils of modern-day slavery or domestic abuse are clear enough, and go beyond this chapter's focus of the subtle daily struggles between right and wrong. There is a greater need to illustrate a typical enemy spy in this cold war of spirituality. Please, beware of this person. Beware of Charm.

The dangers of Charm

Charm is a unique quality for anyone to have, really. It's not as simple as physical beauty or skill at public speaking. Charm is that quality that people possess (in unequal quantities), which elicits trust and appeal in others. Frequently, attractive people possess some Charm automatically. People with at least some popularity, natural authority, and/or assertiveness can be thought of as Charming People. A Charming Person somehow exudes a message that they can be trusted somehow. I speak of Charm here as a neutral quality, for both good people and bad people possess it. Identical Charming twins can use their "trust me" quality for entirely opposite causes or purposes.

Beware of Charm. Charm does not equal goodness, morality, wisdom, or trustworthy. Charm equals Charm. There is nothing else that is quite like it. It has no substitute, and it cannot serve as a substitute for anything else. Charm cannot replace any other quality of a human being. An uninformed person with Charm remains an uninformed person: their opinion is as personal and imperfect as anyone else's. However, their Charm makes their opinion sound more objective and credible - in this way, Charm is an illusion. Beware of being swayed into an unwise opinion backed by a pretty face and a confident voice.

Obviously, not all Charming people are evil manipulators unworthy of our trust or respect. This is not an attack on Charm; rather, it is a warning that Charm sometimes requires an element of caution from us all. When some Charming individual enters our life, we owe it to ourselves to occasionally question our attraction and the ultimate source of our trust. This private audit of credibility is not a betrayal: take courage in the fact that a Charming and truthfully sincere person will stand up to such scrutiny. Honest people can withstand an occasional moment of doubtful concern – despite imperfections. However, to question Charm is be on guard against its abuse, and that is a moment of effort that can prevent great future harm.

The point here, "beware of Charm", is one I make for the sake of spiritual warfare. Cruel and obviously harmful people are typically self-contained, by their abrasive nature and personality. Charming people, on the other hand, can do lasting harm by their façade of trustworthiness. All of us are somewhat more likely to let a Charming person into our lives, even if there are multiple warning signs all along the way. Charm can easily lead to misplaced faith, and misplaced faith is not a good thing in the end.

I offer two personal stories about the problem of Charm. One is about the very beginning of online abuse, in the years preceding the Internet. The other is the unhappy story of a close friend.

A pre-Internet cautionary tale

The story featuring me as the victim is a good lesson, because it separates this idea of Charm from all of its typical associations. This man was able to ooze "trust me" without ever meeting me in person, or divulging any meaningful information about himself, or even relying upon his physical appearance or voice. The mere typed interaction of a primitive chat room was all he really needed, and he forever scarred me in his own minor way. With that background established, on with the story!

Once upon a time, 12-year-old Justin Lopina was exploring the wondrous new worlds of CompuServe and AOL. As I was (and still am) the oldest child of the family, I was the most interested and curious in this new modem-based technology. I registered for an email account years before my brother and sister. I skimmed the horribly-formatted books you could read on your computer screen, as if the library was somehow too passé for me to bother with. A great deal of our bandwidth (was that even the term back then?) was spent downloading jpgs of cast member headshots from Seinfeld and other cutting-edge shows. For anyone ten years younger than me, this probably sounds absolutely horrible. However, I loved it: it was new and exciting, and it was mostly harmless. Unfortunately, this led me into a false sense of security. It didn't take long for me to be excessively trusting of the entire experience.

One night, while fiddling about online, I joined an open and miscellaneous chatroom for the first time. There must have been about fifteen or twenty people there, with nothing but a simple text-to-screen interface. I had a fun time, honestly. I was on for the better part of an hour or so, and the others were kind and interesting. When it was time to log off, I saved the discussion to the hard drive and printed off the entire thing to show my parents.

"Mom! Dad! Look at this! You can type with multiple at the same time: it's the future of communication!" I said, with my eyes gleaming with excitement for the future.

"Wow, Justin. This is pretty cool! So do you know any of these people from anywhere else?" My dad thumbed through the pages, with half of his attention in the pages, and half on my voice.

"No, anyone can log on and join the discussion. In fact, most of the time people log in and out during the same talk."

"Well Justin, it sounds like you're really learning a lot. One of these days you'll have to show us how to go about doing... this... ourselves... Justin?"

"Yeah, dad?" I asked, with some concern, as I suddenly gained my dad's full and complete attention.

"Why did you type all this personal information, here on page 6?"

"Well, it came up..."

"Justin, I'm skimming these pages, and this is not an innocent conversation!" My dad said, not with anger in his voice but significant concern.

"Huh?"

"I've glanced at the whole thing and this is a problem. You're not in trouble, Justin, but your mother and I will have to talk about what to do about this. In the meantime, don't use the computer for anything besides homework."

The parts of the transcript that caught my dad's attention were about 20 minutes into it. Although most of the others were kind and reasonable, one individual had consistently pressured and/or tricked me into giving out personal information. Although some of the others tried to get me to see what was happening, I was far too naive to recognize their words as warnings. By the time I logged out for the night, I had divulged my age, my sex, and my general location as near Milwaukee (although I didn't give my precise address). Along with this information, this person knew my username and therefore could easily acquire my phone number. Even as I went to show off my printouts to my parents, I was totally clueless as to what had just happened: my general instinct to be truthful managed to blind me to suspicious behavior. After my parents read the whole thing more carefully and talked as parents are wont to do, they got a subpoena and succeeded in identifying that person from the chatroom. It was some 40-year-old man, who was not living anywhere near Milwaukee. With confidence that we were not dealing with a legitimate stalking situation, we changed the number of our house phone and got on with life. Thankfully, nothing else happened and whole experience was a relatively minor event in my life. However, I still suspect that my general distrust of the Internet might stem for that one night in the chatroom.

Charm is pretty much its own thing. This man never met me in life. I have no clue what he looked like or sounded like. Even so, he was able to fool me into giving out inappropriate information online. Other people in the chatroom tried to tell me that I did not have to answer his questions, which is proof enough for me that even back then, his behavior was highly suspicious - at least to people with greater common sense than mine when I was 12. Although I don't remember any real details, I do remember the fact that this man *repeatedly* asked me for this information. He was insistent and bold, yet somehow subtle at the same time. In a word, he was Charming in a unique way, and he remains a fine example of why you should beware of Charm. Charm can be sneaky. Charm can win you over, even when onlookers desperately warn you to think twice! How many of us have gotten into a destructive relationship, even as our friends tried and failed to explain why that boyfriend/girlfriend would be a terrible life choice to make?

Charm, in the wrong hands, can be sneaky, subtle, and manipulative. Beware of charm. A good person who happens to be charming will withstand your scrutiny with grace and dignity. So if you are young, consider whether or not to be welcoming to a person into your life because of charm alone. If you are somewhat older and have kids to think about, consider their overall well-being. Sometimes children lack enough common sense to see them through an issue that

107

would be relatively straight-forward for adults. When that happens, it falls to you as parents/teachers/guardians/role models to weed out the problems that are too Charming for your kids to work out themselves. Charm is not always bad. Even so, beware of Charm.

An all-too familiar tale

My second anti-Charm story is far more extreme. Although she told me the story in confidence, she gave me permission to share the overall narrative here. Let's call her Zoe, by virtue of the fact that I don't know anyone by that name. Once upon a time, teenage Zoe started dating as people her own age often do. She met a guy and things went really well for a while. However, things took a dark turn before long. This man became cruel and selfish before long, and sexual abuse was where it all eventually led. This stage of the relationship lasted for a while, until he made the mistake of giving her the visible injury of a black eye. By the time she built up the courage to completely cut him out of her life, her sense of self-worth had been permanently scarred: she had been beaten, berated, and neglected. One of the many acts of sexual abuse led to pregnancy which ended in abortion, which of course led to other negative consequences down the line.

Zoe's story, at least up to this point, is not terribly uncommon. Women somehow manage to get locked into such relationships with alarming ease, and escaping such harmful people is far more difficult than anyone can imagine – at least until you've had to go through that experience yourself. A while back, I watched the Netflix series Jessica Jones because of my friends' recommendation of it. Although the show didn't seem all that interesting to me personally, my friends raved about how emotionally powerful it was: a superheroine story entirely based on an emotionally abusive relationship. To directly quote a female friend of mine,

"Jessica Jones was an intense and engaging show because it summed up all my greatest fears of being a straight and unmarried woman." Although, in my opinion, men react to abusive relationships in different ways, they suffer from the same cause: an abusive person within an intimate relationship.

That said, Zoe specifically belongs in this chapter because of the continuing aftermath. You see, Zoe's abuser was the absolute classic example of a Charming man. He was seemingly able to get people to instantly like him and trust him. He was confident, funny, and bold – people respond positively to such qualities. Zoe would occasionally find herself in a position where she could bear to explain at least a part of her emotional toil and despair. She would open up to a friend or two, or to her parents. More often than not, her listeners simple would not believe her! They would give half-assed explanations (read: excuses), or simple platitudes. It is true that many people do not know how to properly communicate with someone who's hurting – it's a skill that requires some training. However, Zoe's frustrations went beyond that because these friends and family of hers knew her abuser. They knew him and they liked him. They did not want to face the reality that he was not the person they assumed he was. Therefore, they tried to offer other ways of looking at what happened. They'd talk to Zoe about overreacting or projecting her own insecurities onto him. They'd remind her of how good her abuser was at one time or another. Perhaps they even made the mistake of telling her that she didn't really understand what she was feeling.

When Zoe and I talked about this, those reactions were a major part of our discussion. Zoe's friends and family did not take her pleas for help seriously. They could not or would not see her recent past as something truly devastating; they could not or would not see her as someone in profound need of compassion and understanding. Rather, they saw her as an immature girl with ex-boyfriend angst. For Zoe, that utter lack of empathy in her life was heartbreaking. A heartbreak stacked upon a heartbreak, in essence.

I hope and believe that Zoe is better now, with at least a few more good influences in her life. Her abuser is far away and firmly in her past, and the fact that she made the time to talk to me about all this is itself a sign that she is choosing to deal with these traumas rather than to suppress them. Make no mistake: Zoe knows spiritual warfare – she's been in the trenches and lost in No Man's Land. She's been battered and broken, with no recourse but to crawl back on her own to the closest thing she had to a safe place. Zoe has dozens, if not hundreds, of people in her life; the people who know at least a part of what she's been through can be counted on one hand. That's what makes it spiritual warfare: the vast bulk of the struggle is within one's own private life, and even a single genuine ally is a major advantage. So often, it would seem, we find ourselves entirely on our own and wonder how long we can hold out.

Fear of the future

This reflection upon spiritual warfare leads to a somewhat related topic: the fear of the future. We all fight our personal battles. We fight to preserve the faith in our skeptical family members, we fight against negative influences, and we fight against the injustice we happen to witness. Still, when respite comes, we tend to look at the big picture. We look at the state of the world, or the state of the church, or even the state of the family. We look at how difficult life can be, and how easily we can fail to stand up and pass on the most important parts of our lives. When those moments come, we get afraid. Everyone, in their own way, fears for the future. The nature of spiritual warfare makes such fears an absolute necessity. Guarantees for goodness are rare, and the next threat against the things we hold dear is always apparently imminent.

Between my education and my experience, I only have a minor reflection to pass here and now: the future is never as bleak as it seems. We always fret over our losses. When a Cradle Catholic falls away from the faith in 8th grade, we are naturally saddened by that news. Parents are devastated at such a turn of events, and that 8th grader's priests, teachers, and relatives are also saddened by the news. We hear such a thing, and we assume the world itself is crumbling around us.

Still, we tend to ignore the victory stories. The stories about faith winning out in the end, or the stories about some kind of imminent future gloom that fails to take root in reality. In short, my message is this, with respect to the fear of the future: the worthwhile parts of life are inherently stable. With respect to our future, the means to its continuation will present themselves. Those means may not present themselves in the way that we want or expect, but they most certainly are there.

God is absolutely present in the world today: I've seen him at work. God is in no real danger. The notion of faith, as an element to ordinary daily life, is no real danger. The Catholic Church, as a vehicle to salvation, is in no real danger. Could we be facing a future with fewer priests and fewer churches? Yes, that is a possibility. Could we be facing a world where the faithful are more marginalized than they are now? Yes, those times of oppression are absolutely nothing new. However, even in the face of whatever hardship awaits us as a community united in the belief that we are loved beyond all knowing, everything good and necessary will continue by the grace of the Holy Spirit. I assert this here and now, despite being aware that religious observance is dwindling in our part of the world. Even in light of growing skepticism, apathy, and general confusion, God will provide for his creation. He will provide for all the needs here present, and that includes the presence of a Faithful Remnant: a core group of believers that keep

111

faith and conviction alive in an era of lax devotion and insipid values. After all, attitudes of lax devotion and insipid values don't last - they only thrive during periods of immaturity. As people grow into something greater, their appreciation for more subtle virtues grow as well. The act of praying the rosary will never make much sense to people who cannot spare 20 minutes of their day to prayer. However, once the addiction to one's work or smartphone wears off a bit, the worth of silence and focused thought will certainly dawn upon them. So if someone in your life is afraid for the future, please remind them on my behalf that the future is more stable than it seems. As periods of immaturity give way to periods of greater respect and wisdom, so periods of hardship will give way to ones of prosperousness. We need only remain patient in times of famine, grateful in times of feasting, and consistent with all things truly worthy of our time.

Counterattacks (for our side!)

The good news is that there are counterattacks at work in the world, for the side of all people of good will. With respect to our fear of the future, as a natural thing that affects many of us, the point made in the previous paragraphs is the most central: consistency is key, with respect to all things deserving our time and energy. The mere refusal of quitting counts for more than we give it credit for. That stated, being on the winning side of spiritual warfare is not simply holding down the fort as long as our strength holds out. In the midst of all our daily struggles and predictable occurrences, good surprises do happen to us. Amen, amen, I say to you: God loves surprises. Or at the very least, he likes messing with us. I leave it to the reader to decide which one is the more accurate statement.

When the big and directly beneficial surprises come to my attention, I tend to think of them as Spiritual Warfare Counterattacks. We sometimes feel under attack by something (or someone), and it is easy to begin seeing the world as a darker place as a result. These counterattacks are essentially the moments when the world gets brighter, seemingly all on its own. To be clear, I'm not advocating improvements to reality, free of human choice or involvement, as if God is somehow in the practice of fine-tuning the key and specific decisions of people at opportune times. If that were the case, it would probably sound like a series of fast-acting possessions by the Holy Spirit... I doubt that it works that way, to say the least. Rather, when I say "seemingly all on its own", I mean that goodness and success can sometimes catch us off-guard. We can be taken aback by a triumph that was entirely independent of our awareness. Of course, those triumphs exist for a reason, even if we fail to see them coming. We might very well be a part of the process - after all, we often influence and inspire others in life, without any knowledge of said contribution. With that context in mind, I sincerely hope *everyone* is able to have faith that someone in the world is better, happier, and/or braver because of one's presence in their life.

So what does a counterattack look like? It's truly a question with no objective answer - any response *must* be subjective and tailored toward the subject's own life and values. However, there are perhaps a few examples that are clearer than others.

One counterattack that has not entirely borne fruit yet is my friend's consideration for the permanent deaconate. He hasn't gone through with it yet, and will not be able to do so for several more years, but the very consideration is enough for celebration. You see, Joe and I were in CCD together in middle school: religious formation classes for those who did not attend Catholic school. As a matter of fact, it was a central factor of how we met in the first place in 6th grade. Now, the volunteers who served as once-a-week teachers for us did not highly regard us. Joe was the perpetual class clown, to the point where he was almost a cliché. I intend to tell

113

my best story about him for the rest of my life! One Wednesday night, Joe brought an entire backpack to religion class. In this backpack, Joe had several copies of a comic book - the *same exact copy*. During the inevitable period of class where we to read along in our Bibles, Joe took out a comic book and began to read it over his opened Bible. The teacher saw this, walked over to him, and took his comic book away. Then, a minute later, Joe took out another comic book, opened it to the last page he was reading, and continued along his way. He did this for at least three comic books! After that, my memory is a bit fuzzy. Several of us were suppressing massive laughter all the while, and he remains to this day an absolute legend among that peer group!

Of course, I was not all that much better. Where Joe was funny above all, I was the perpetual questioner who never really accepted the easy answers. My constant inquisitive nature was well-documented by many. I had no idea of the effect that I had on them, for the better part of a decade. It only hit me when I volunteered to be a church catechist when I was 25 or so. As is typical for these sorts of things, we had a beginning-of-the-school-year meeting to get on the same page and have some basic orientation. Bless her heart, my first-grade religion teacher was still teaching and astoundingly still remembered me! To this day, I'm still a bit shocked by her greeting:

"I can't believe it's you! Mr. Lopina, I'm so glad that you're here and going to teach. All those years when you were a boy, we thought you were an atheist!"

Now this greeting threw me off. I've certainly had moments of "which religion is best for me?", but I've never turned away from God entirely. It was an odd statement.

"Why did you think I was an atheist?"

"Because you asked too many questions!"

I can't remember that moment clearly anymore; I can't remember whether or not I burst

out laughing at that very moment. In my memory, there was certainly boisterous laughter.

However I initially reacted, we had a good laugh and that year of my life was one of my best

transition years: years which I mainly spent preparing for my next major adventure (in this case,

waiting for my Peace Corps application to go through). After I had some time to reflect a bit on

what my old teacher said, I realized that she did, in fact, have good reason for thinking what she

did. I remembered an ancient classroom moment, way back in 1st grade.

"And that, kids, is when Jesus ascended to heaven."

"What does that mean?"

"That was went Jesus went directly to heaven without dying."

"Um, what did that look like?"

"Oh, well Jesus rose up to heaven while floating on a cloud."

Although I was far too polite of a kid to say it out loud, I'm quite certain that my face said

it all: "Oh come on, you just made that up!"

So, with that little backdrop into our childhoods, here's the point for spiritual warfare: we

might very well have been the least likely people to take Holy Orders. Holy Orders is the

Sacramental term for becoming a deacon, priest, or bishop. It is a formal declaration that your

life belongs to Christ and the Church, and Holy Orders are permanent: once a priest, forever a priest. With respect to Joe and me, of our entire class at that church, we are the only two people who have seriously considered Holy Orders. Obviously, mine are solid now that I'm well over two years into my priesthood. At the time of this writing, Joe has not yet taken steps toward the permanent deaconate. He's married (with three kids), and not as financially stable as he'd like. However, in the near future, Joe may very well be a permanent deacon and serve the church as best he can in his off hours. He could occasionally preach at Mass, visit with the sick or imprisoned, assist with baptisms, weddings, or funerals, or otherwise give his parish aid wherever he could. If that happens, I will be filled with glee and I will absolutely be there to welcome him on his ordination day. However, even if that never happens, it means a lot to me that he's seriously considered it. The both of us have come a long way, and the odds were certainly against us.

The way I see it, our attraction to Holy Orders is a kind of counterattack in the spiritual warfare we all find ourselves in. At its core, it was not a gradual thing. In a way, it *became* a gradual thing over time as I discerned and prayed about priesthood throughout college and Peace Corps and seminary. It was not something that was nurtured or defended or planned for at its definitive moment. It... just... happened. It wasn't magic, and I'm fairly confident that the Holy Spirit didn't possess me for a time. The consideration of Holy Orders did happen for a reason, but it was a reason that was totally unexpected when it first appeared.

I read somewhere, too long ago to hope to quote the exact book, that the initial seizing of an idea is called a "eureka moment". Such times happen to everyone somehow: we find ourselves facing a problem with no clue to how to proceed. It need not be rocket science; the problem could be simple housework, the final paragraph of a wedding reception speech, or what

116

to do about a conflict of personality in the classroom or office. As suddenly as a flash of lightning, a fantastic new idea sometimes hits us in our cluelessness.

"Ah! Eureka! Try the plunger first!"

"Of course! Bill and Angela perfectly reflect their families by their culinary styles, don't they?"

"How didn't I see it before? Sam and Jason have been fighting all year, only now Elizabeth is in the middle of it all."

At that precise moment, the new information just hits you, and it is not something that was nurtured or planned or expected. It just pops into your head. However, once the idea is there, it can be interacted with. It can then be nurtured and developed and used to plan future endeavors. Still, for all that planning to take place, there first be a personal moment of pure, unbridled discovery. In such a way, some great things begin with a "eureka moment".

Good things can seemingly pop into reality. Perhaps more often than we give them credit for, the values of goodness and justice launch a counterattack. We need to recognize the good things often come without warning. If we make the mistake of looking at the world and assuming the worst, we do not merely fail to see the goodness around us. We lose our ability to act wisely, in light of these surprises. True insights can surprise us at the moment of their big reveal. Men and women can prove to be great parents, in spite of the way lived while single. A large donation to a good cause can come at an opportune time. A friend can makes the right choice at the 11th hour, with our well-being hanging in the balance. The future is never as bleak as it first seems. Good things do happen, and they often happen without warning. Keep an eye out for them.

The bottom line.

Here's where things get tricky... I would be remiss to end the chapter on that simple high note, because spiritual warfare is not simple or straightforward. If anything, spiritual warfare is tricky and deceptive at its heart. Some struggles in life are concrete and measurable: a financial struggle, for instance, is as quantifiable as anything can be. Some challenges at work can be dependent on certain tasks being achieved on time. Spiritual warfare, by contrast, is fluid and difficult to entirely grasp. When did it truly begin? When will it all be over? What is the best way to move forward? These are typical questions for one contemplating this particular aspect of life.

The subjective element of our thinking is certainly a part of spiritual warfare, and perhaps provides us with our own worst enemies - so often, our efforts of fighting against one another are done with the exact same goal (albeit by different names) in mind. A friend of mine from Peace Corps was a real joy to be with while in Africa. She was funny and kind, and always good for cheering up your day. However, she also had a few opinions and values that deeply offended me, such as her denial of the value of spirituality and faith in one's life. A shallow person might assume that the two of us would be mortal enemies in the long run, on account of several conflicting values: wouldn't the two of us spend our lives attempting to achieve opposite goals? I don't believe so. Now that our time in Africa is at an end, she fights for the well-being of the most underprivileged children in the United States. She amazes me. I find her personality astoundingly complex and I know that she is doing her best. I know that she's not passive and selfish like so many others - she truly does want to make the world a better place, and she's willing to face down dangerous people to do it. So... where is she, in terms of spiritual warfare? Is she on the side of goodness or not? Perhaps the answer isn't an easy one to qualitatively express, but my gut certainly tells me that she has far more goodness in her than not. This friend and fellow volunteer taught me that there are no clear boundaries or dividing lines as we go about that perpetual struggle of truth, justice, and freedom. Enemies become allies, weaknesses becomes strengths, and uncertainty becomes its own sort of knowledge. Such is life. Such is the most important facet of life. Such are the conditions we find ourselves in when our decisions and actions matter the most.

There is one final complication that bears clarification: the subjective element of morality. Some of the examples and experiences in this chapter could be viewed as an argument for relativism or some other purely subjective worldview. For the record, that is not the origin or goal of this thought process. I philosophically consider myself a transubjective objectivist. That means that I believe that human beings have varying opinions and values with respect to morality and other abstract concepts such as beauty, freedom, or kindness. However, while that subjective nature of human thought must always be respected, there nevertheless remains an objective and unchanging truth underlying it all. To use an analogy, I believe that no two human beings will ever have precisely the same taste in art. One person will favor impressionism, the other neo-cubism. That is a subjective difference in opinion. Nevertheless, they both value the beauty and inspiration that art has to offer - even if their particular styles have nothing else in common whatsoever. Hence, with abstract concepts or personal values, there is a mix of objective and subjective elements at work. It is right and just to seek out the good, even as we all approach it out in our own individual style.

Understand the true bottom line: the willingness to admit that spiritual warfare is a reality is to admit that a meaningful struggle between right and wrong can be covert, subtle, and open-ended. It is paradoxically an objective reality and a subjective perception. Thus, some of our best work as people is done with no witnesses, no payoff, and no known finishing point. Some of our most horrid moments in life, as a result of spiritual warfare, can weary us because no one can fully understand the fight we're in. This fight is worthwhile. This refusal to let the world be inherited by the wrong people is bravery incarnate and faith-in-action. Steel yourself, and believe in your ability to know what is right and just. Most of the time, you won't be wrong.

Chapter Ten: Respect: The Quintessential

Value of Civilization

"Ksitigarbha" in Sanskrit means "to hold the world within," and like the great earth, Jizō

Bosatsu has an unwavering heart in the intention to save all sentient beings.

-Buddhist Statuary: A Bilingual Guide to Japan, Ishii Ayako

At the time of this writing, I intended for this to be the final chapter of my first book

because it is probably the unexpected lesson I have to offer after two years of priesthood. In

brief, respect is a quality and a behavior that absolutely everyone ought to have in some

measure. Respect - true, lasting, and genuine respect - transcends culture, language, religion, lack of religion, and personality. Where respect is lacking, hurtfulness, callousness, selfishness, and intimidation are sure to follow. Where respect is lacking, bullies thrive and multiply. After two years of priesthood, I am in a unique position to make this claim with the whole of my being. I spend a good amount of time with people who have no real faith to speak of. On the other hand, as a diocesan priest, I spend a great deal of my time with practicing Catholics as well as non-practicing Catholics who happen to be in enough spiritual need to give me a call or drop by my office.

Across the board, no matter the professed religion nor the amount of faith therein, respect is always the key factor. A kind atheist is far better company than a cruel Catholic, and vice versa. It is so easy to pray with people when they actively desire my presence and want to express their faith. Even if they've been away from the Church for so long, and they can't manage the Lord's Prayer on their own, the time of prayer will be meaningful and beautiful – because the mere desire to gather together in time of need is enough.

By contrast, no amount of orthodox teaching will discount or justify the emotional damage left behind by threats or inappropriate complaints. At the time of this writing, the emotional damage of an approximate eighteen-month period of service has succeeded at impeding my ministry to its very core. If I look back at those individual moments of disrespect and cruelty, it seems reasonable that most people do not entirely realize how harmful they truly are to others. Perhaps the matter is cyclical: hurt people hurt people. People get hurt at some point, and therefore complain and harass others with aggression as a result. From there, those actions cause more hurt, which leads to continued intimidation and anger. If that is the case, then genuine respect is the key to breaking that cycle of hurt and pain.

This universal need for respect, a need we all experience, may shed light on why so many Americans are so miserable overall. During my travels in life, I have not visited a country with less overall respect than the United States. While I'm confident that such a country probably exists, I haven't encountered it yet: American culture has somehow made us petty and callous. I do not believe this attitude of disrespect has anything to do with American faith (or lack thereof), or that it is associated with any particular demographic. Rather, I see the problem as a holistic one: it applies to the whole.

Now, as a lifelong Catholic, I've long been afraid to express my faith openly - it's a fear that I still have today. The primary reason for it has been the consistent shaming I've received from people of every walk of life. After a while, the hurtfulness just doesn't seem worth the trouble. While in seminary, I had to force myself to put a cross on my jacket's lapel. Even though I understood that I would eventually be wearing a clerical collar, the prospect of wearing a piece of my faith terrified me in some small but real way.

That fear affects me today, and it saddens me. It saddens me that people feel free to lash out at others with an ease that appears to be little more than flippant impulsiveness. It saddens me, because I actually do understand people's frustrations with the Catholic Church. If they brought their pains to my attention in a different way, they would almost certainly find a true ally and sympathetic ear in me. I wish that happened more often; I wish we had the ability to express our angers and doubts in a more civilized way. Simple respect really can be the key to that civilized way.

Can I prove that the problem is mainly an American one? Certainly not, at least not by way of deductive logic. It is more of an inductive conclusion made by way of personal experience. In the recent past, I have traveled to Israel, the Dominican Republic, Haiti, Burkina

123

Faso, Columbia, and Japan. For all of these trips (apart from my Peace Corps service in Burkina Faso), I was either a seminarian or priest: a Catholic man of faith. Although I did not go to these countries for active ministry, my faith was certainly a part of who I was. For each country I had the pleasure of seeing and living in, I never experienced crushing disrespect at the hands of anyone overseas. Even during my terrifying 48 hours in Haiti (where my language skills were meager at best), I could be myself in ways that would be quite difficult in America. Even as an entire village of Haitian children gathered to watch me read a book and drink a beer while I waited for a friend to meet me, I was never mocked for who I was or what I believed. Not even the bizarre color of my skin could change that. I walked freely in my clerical collar in the streets of Cartagena, Columbia... and it felt great to do so. Such a feeling for me in America is possible, but somewhat rare.

Of course, Haiti and the Dominican Republic are two nations with a large Catholic presence, and although profoundly few Christians live in Israel, Christian pilgrims are perfectly common. Hence, those countries would not be difficult for any priest to feel at least somewhat at home. That leaves us with Burkina Faso and Japan, where witnessing faith may be easier said than done. As a matter of fact, one reason some friends and family didn't want me to go to Africa for my Peace Corps experience was the simple fact that Burkina Faso is approximately 50% Muslim. The concern for my safety was brought up more than once.

Even with the concerns of my family and friends in mind, I was truly excited to go to a Muslim country for an extended period of time. Besides the fact that I had always known that most Muslims are peace-loving and perfectly ordinary people, I was also aware that Burkina Faso was a remarkably peaceful country overall. So I saw the assignment as a once-in-a-lifetime opportunity to live among Muslims with no real fear of danger or anti-Christian hatred. Sadly, those insights of 2005/2006 are no longer as true. Since my return to the states in 2008, Burkina Faso has grown in civil unrest with an increase of anti-American and anti-European terrorist activity. At the time of this writing, there was is a Peace Corps presence in the county, but it is limited to the safer and more Christian two-thirds of the country. The northern third of the country, where I was assigned, is currently considered off-limits to all Peace Corps volunteers for their own safety.

Nevertheless, 2006-2008 was a great period of time to be an American in West Africa. Right off the bat, it's worth noting that West Africa doesn't have a great deal of anti-American sentiment. Their colonizing country was France; therefore France and Western Europe gets the majority of the animosity of the Burkinabe (a blanket term for citizens of Burkina Faso, regardless of ethnicity). My group of 33 volunteers spent three months together in training, and then we were assigned to our individual villages for the two years of active service. Of those 33 possible assignments, only two of them were available to me and in the desert-like north. So during my placement interview, I specifically mentioned that I wanted to live in a desert environment and have some exposure to Islamic daily life. The Peace Corps administrator responsible for placement did a short "happy dance" for that. As it turned out, my location was one of the hardest ones to fill, and no one else particularly wanted it. A win-win scenario for all 33 of us, as well as the administrator. So as of late August of 2006, I was officially placed in Gorgadji: a northern village of about 2000 people – a medium town by Burkina standards, with plenty of Muslims, a Protestant church, and a small Catholic church. I was grateful for that breakdown of demographic; my only complaint was our lack of a priest. A French priest assigned to the nearest large town would cycle through our villages for major events like Ash Wednesday. However, we were on our own for typical Sundays.

Shortly after my arrival, I began getting to know the Muslim population as best as I could. By a stroke of luck, a fellow American named Jen was assigned to my village with me, and she lived with a Muslim family on the other side of town. So I would often come to her house to hang out and speak English, and we would practice our French with her family. For our first year, we would sit in her courtyard and watch the family pray during Ramadan. After some time passed, Jen's host father would occasionally take me to pray in a local Mosque with his particular part of the Islamic community. To this day, I hold great respect for Islamic prayer styles, and their devotion to consistently pray each and every day at the appropriate time. Whenever I would join them, it was plainly understood that I was a practicing Catholic and that there was absolutely no chance of converting me to their faith. Still, they treated me as one of their own and tolerated the fact that I didn't know any of the prayers apart from the absolute basics. It was enough for us all that I was there and doing my best to mimic those around me, with respect.

Naturally, things were far from perfect as far as my attempt to accept and understand African culture and religion. Above and beyond all other things, I couldn't stand Koranic schools wherever I found them (which was practically everywhere). A Koranic school is a small Islamic educational system typically found in minor villages. Students there learn nothing but how to read the Koran: their holy book. So these children grow up with absolutely no exposure to mathematics, other literature, science, critical thinking, or history. I never once saw these schools as even remotely capable of substituting for an ordinary education in a public school. Even if school was costly for a typical family beyond the fifth grade, those five grades of proper development were priceless by comparison. As a result of the culture's general disinterest in education overall, it is now a country where you might easily encounter a shopkeeper who is incapable of basic addition and subtraction, and cannot read or write beyond signing their name.

All that said, for everything that I witnessed and disliked, I always felt safe and respected overall. Gorgadji was my village and my home; although I was obviously an outsider, I was an honored guest and (temporary) member of the community. The differences of our faiths, and the ways that they impacted society, were not enough to break down the essential fraternity between people of good will. As we read in Psalm 133, verse 1: "Behold, how good it is, and how pleasant, where brethren dwell as one!" As I look back on those years in Africa, I truly miss the sense of simple peace I had when in village. That simple sense of community was easily taken for granted at the moment, but it seems a precious treasure now, a decade later.

As it so happens, the funniest joke told at my expense was by a Muslim in village. I went to church on Sunday morning, somewhat on the northern outskirts of town. By random chance, that Sunday was Market Day. As Market Day was every third day, it would fall on a Sunday as often as any other day of the week. As I left the church, I walked back to town as a group of perhaps twenty people were going the same way to sell their fruits and vegetables in the market. Most of them couldn't speak French, but one man (perhaps 40 years old?) struck up a conversation as we walked together. We chatted about church, and his Mosque in his home village. As we neared my home, which was closer than the market, what he said next is forever sealed in my memory.

"Thank you for talking. You are a nice man!"

"Thank you. You are a nice man too."

"No, no. You don't understand. You are a *very* nice man... You should marry my mom!" As he said that, he gestured to a 70-year-old-or-so lady a few steps behind us. She almost certainly didn't know what we were saying, but may have understood the joke by way of non-verbal communication and context. As I stood there, dumbfounded at what was just said, she looked at me, smiled, and revealed her two remaining teeth (as stereotypically crooked and yellow as could be). I think I muttered something like "no thanks, I'm fine" before splitting off to my courtyard. Be assured that there was much laughter from me and the group at our moment of passing.

One final memory is worth sharing, by way of the sense of welcome I received in a non-Christian community: my very last full day in Gorgadji. I was all packed and ready to go; I was going to visit other volunteers around the country before flying home to the states, but my time in village came to an end with the closing of the academic school year. As such, I decided that it would be a friendly gesture to go to mosque one last time and offer my thanks to the Muslim community for the last two years. The timing was appropriate, as it had been several months since I had actively taken part in anything involving the villagers – the final months of Peace Corps requires a fair amount of paperwork away from village, and once completed, I had final exams to give out and correct. So I went with Jen's host father, who had been a good friend for my entire stay. He spoke the village's local language as well as French, so he came with me for moral support and to translate: many people at the mosque couldn't speak French, including the Imam (their equivalent of a priest/religious leader).

At the end of prayer time, I expressed my thanks. In response, the Imam rapidly and passionately spoke in his native language. He gesticulated toward me and Jen's host father repeatedly, and spoke for a full thirty seconds. For that whole time, I was almost frozen in fear because he sounded angry and upset. In my mind, I was translating his words according to his gestures and intonation: "How presumptuous is this American? How could you do this to us,

[Jen's host father]? How dare you bring this white person into our sacred space? What is wrong with you?" After he was done, with my heart pounding at about double its ordinary rate, Jen's host father leaned over to me and said "He's very happy that you came to pray with us." After a couple final laughs and firm handshakes, we all parted ways for the last time. I'll never forget how well I was treated, from my first day to my last, in spite of living in a culture that was so obviously different from my own.

Japan is probably not compared to West Africa too often. However, in their differing ways, they can offer about the same degree of culture shock to a typical American. An older cousin of mind lived in Japan for a number of years for business purposes, and hated just about every day he spent there. In short, it was not his kind of place to live and be happy; from Japan, he moved to England, which suited him well. He now has dual citizenship and permanently resides there. When the two of us get together, we often reflect on how different we are with respect to our favored foreign nations and cultures. While I can't precisely describe why I enjoy Japan so much, a partial answer is the prevailing attitude of basic respect that exists there. Although I only stayed there for two weeks, I went with the specific goal of immersing myself in the language and culture as much as possible. Every single day included at least one significant conversation, with most of them involving the sequence of questions that I've come to know as an "introduction conversation". It's like a warm-up before getting in to more advanced conversation topics. Most introduction conversations follow the same pattern, with each person asking and answering the same questions:

"Hello, how are you?"

"What is your name?"

"Do you live here?"

"Do you work here?"

"How old are you?"

"What are you drinking?"

"How was the weather for you today?"

"How is the family?"

You get the idea. Well, for these little talks, I never brought up faith in the conversation - I wouldn't have done so, even if I had the requisite vocabulary. However, my conversation partners would often ask what my job was, and I told the truth. Most of the time, they would assume that the heard me incorrectly. After a few signs of the cross and a couple of pictures of me at church (and a few laughs on the side), they'd get the idea. At least during my trip to Japan, I never got a bad reaction as a result of my vocation. Everyone I spoke with was interested, curious, and joyful with respect to my priestliness. Due to the lack of vocabulary, I never had an in-depth conversation about religion, which was fine with me. However, what little we did talk about was discussed openly between equals. I never had to defend myself or apologize for some crime of others in the past, or even explain what brought me to this life as opposed to a "normal" profession. It was such a relief to experience that! It was genuinely encouraging to say such things out loud without the fear of accusations or insults. In fact, most Japanese people think about the notion of faith differently than Americans and Europeans do. The religions that the Japanese typically adhere to require very little devotion (compared to the expectation of attending church every Sunday), and they are not solely about faith: respect is also a major aspect in of itself. Although there is probably an advanced and credible source out there to back

that claim up, I'd like to offer a down-to-earth reference instead.

Hiragana Times is a magazine for English speakers who are studying the Japanese

language. In the January 2016 issue, one Q&A article was "Who is Worshiped at Shrines?" It

was a timely article, because the New Year sees heavy traffic at temples. The most significant

portion of the article was near the end, when the issue of enshrined class A war criminals from

World War II came up. Should such war criminals be allowed to be enshrined? Or can they be

respected and honored as any other soldier who died for their country?

There are members of congress and other people who say that visiting the shrine is an

internal issue and a question of personal choice, and that it is only natural that the nation

and its citizens display respect for those who died for their country. Putting this into

context is the Japanese view of life and death; that the dead cannot be blamed after they

pass away. (Hiragana Times, Jan 2016, pg 27)

That was a fascinating read. Put simply, Japan has chosen to retain the ability and

availability to show respect to their dead. Even in light of all the horror and shame that may

have arisen from World War II, the desire to maintain a level of respect and dignity for all people

remains strong and everlasting. The dead are to be remembered, for who they were. The time

for blame, judgment, and anger has come and gone. The dead are beyond such things, and the

living owe them a degree of that freedom from the discrimination of history. How many of our

American dead would benefit from such an attitude?

Honestly, I find that concept intriguing, fascinating, and potentially very useful with respect to keeping one's religion an active part of a cultural identity. In Japan, the structure is in place for everyone and anyone to take part in religious devotion, no matter where they stood in terms of spirituality and overall belief. There is work to be done by the truly faithful and those dedicated to the cause. There are places of genuine sanctity for those in need, and there are welcome places for people to go for fun and periodic and simple participation. I witnessed this, and I couldn't help but consider the long-term effects of that arrangement. Religious activity was open to absolutely anyone, no matter their motives or affiliations: a French tourist could appreciate a prayer garden alongside Japanese youth enjoying the fresh air, with some older folks lost in their mediations a few feet away. Everyone was there in a state of simple harmony, and I wish it were possible to take that environment and feeling back home when it was time to leave. Such are the fruits of unconditional respect.

What if a place like Japan has managed to instill the idea of respect upon its people? What if that personal and communal respect serves as a natural buffer against hatred and cruelty during their daily lives? And what if that respect and lack of hatred eventually lead to the attitude that one's personal life of faith was one's own business without eliminating the presence of communal and social devotion? Would such a culture be entirely alien to Christ's wishes? I sincerely doubt that would be the case... In fact, I believe that Christ smiles upon such countries. Even with the understanding that I am probably idolizing Japanese culture to a certain extent, the fact remains that my faith was something my Japanese hosts were easily able to celebrate and appreciate on its own merits. That spiritual generosity is something America is in dire need of - we as Americans need that simple brotherliness far more than Japan needs churches.

Church culture, in Catholic America, is an odd community overall. While it's the only religious environment I really know all that well, others have been quite happy to explain that their denominations have a fairly similar dynamic within their community. On the one hand, parishes are communities that gather in faith and good will. Parishes ought to be kind and supportive and welcoming, in all things. Indeed, most parishes are all of those things some of the time, ideally most of the time. Churches make special effort to welcome new people on Sunday mornings. They seek to aid the poor and the downtrodden. There are groups that meet in good faith, and there really is something for everyone at a typical parish. These are all good things.

However, at the same time, parishes can be strangely cruel to the very people they seek to serve. Perhaps naturally, clothing and hairstyles will be judged by way of whispers and dirty looks. Just as naturally, people will complain about the parish not being liberal enough or not conservative enough, or not [insert personal value here] enough.

On a different level, however, a parish can be cruel and petty in more subtle ways. Passive-aggressive approaches to problems are as common as bake sales. Bullies seem to thrive in parishes, and I believe that most parishes have something of an "in crowd" within it. When you add it up, you get a profoundly complicated result. You get a place, and a people associated with that place, that wavers between "saintly respectful" and "despicably disrespectful". A church is its own sort of microcosm: a small reality that somehow echoes the truths that can be found in the greater realities of daily life and the real world. Those realities might regard the absolute necessity of all ages coming together in community, the nature of financial stability, or the unending competition between various special interest groups. Whatever the case may be, if the parish in question has its share of respect, the micro-reality of the church can be educational and illustrate how things ought to operate elsewhere in life. By contrast, if the parish in question has less than its share of respect, it will most likely serve as a cautionary tale. After all, a community of faith with a lack of respect is not likely to be financially affluent in the long-term. Nor will it be effectively integrated between ages, demographics, or interests. Such a church will surely need some drastic change in its future, in order to re-establish its true mission of the salvation of souls. The salvation of souls, at least in the context of organized religion, is a facet of civilization. And respect is civilization's quintessential value.

Chapter 11: Two Years of Reflection,

but Ten Years of Growth

It was a bleak land, a bleak house. Fire roared in the deep hearth, giving as always more

warmth for the eye and spirit than for the flesh, for the stone floor and walls, the wind

outside blowing down off the mountains and the Ice, drank up most of the heat of the

flames. But I did not feel the cold as I used to, my first two years on Winter; I had lived

long in a cold land, now.

-*The Left Hand of Darkness*, Ursula K. Le Guin

The whole point of this book was to offer a tidbit of wisdom by way of the last two years

of life: the first two years of priesthood. Perhaps some would consider them cold years: time spent in the service of a local community that I would never truly belong to. Perhaps that does indeed make up the stone floor and walls of life, slammed with hard lessons like a bitterly cold wind. Should that be true on some level, there remains a hearthfire, which warms the soul. We learn from the harsh lessons of life, and we grow as we cope with the bad news. While I can apply that idiom to myself, it can apply to just about anyone. However, upon reflection of this last decade, perhaps my mother is the one who's changed the most through adversity.

To be fair, the reflection didn't start with my mom but with my fellows from Peace Corps. June 8th, 2016 was the ten-year anniversary of my departure for Burkina Faso, Africa, and my whole group was quick to celebrate online by way of shared pictures and memories. We had agreed for service in the Peace Corps for two years and three months, which I successfully completed with the exception of one three-week vacation back to the states. My group, thirty three people in all, became known as the "hard corps" group. Out of our entire group, we only lost four people to early release-of-service; the educational group after us lost more than half of their numbers before over their two years were completed. Ten of us (I was not among their number) requested a third year of service, three of them were accepted for that extra term. We took our work seriously and supported one another as best as we could. After teaching 6th - 8th grade math and science for two academic years, I was entirely ready to head back home.

On June 8th, 2016, I spent the entire day reflecting on the past decade of my life. How far had I come? What was the same? What was different? I was absolutely glowing with nostalgia, because it was so terribly easy to be thankful for that kind of life experience. I miss each and every one of my fellow volunteers that I served with. I miss my simple house in the middle of the desert; I miss celebrating absolutely everything by drinking and dancing with any other volunteers that happened to be in that city at that time; and I even miss the dust storms that tore my electronics to shreds. I still proudly travel with the same hiking backpack, and I've told friends and family to never gift me real luggage: I'll just return it or give it away. I still decorate my lodgings like my home in Burkina; I still nap after lunch when possible (which is an excellent habit in an absurdly hot environment); and I try to celebrate a rainstorm the way I did all those years ago when rain was rare.

My two years of priesthood have been more important than my two years of Peace Corps. As a teacher, I was adequate. Three of my students went on to college after my departure, but I'm quite sure they would have gone with or without me in their lives. Although I learned French well during training, it failed to improve in any meaningful measure during my years of service due to the simplistic French spoken in the villages. As a priest, I was more than adequate for at least some of the time. There were grace-filled moments happening every month of my life, if not every week. The people closest to me, the people who were truly in need of something, have made it clear that our lives truly do intersect and depend on one another. Still, even if 2014 - 2016 was a more humanistically successful time, 2006 - 2008 was the foundation for it. Those years in Gorgadji, Burkina Faso gave me the time to think that I needed. It provided self-confidence, the chance to live a new language beyond the classroom, the challenge to survive on one's own, and it illuminated the sheer joy of service: the pleasure that comes with living with a genuine and righteous purpose that remains present each and every day. Even when things were rough, that joy was still there in the background of my mind.

It's cool to look back on a large chunk of time (at least for me, ten years counts as a large chunk) and know that the time was used wisely. Who would I be now without those years away from home? Shortly before my departure in 2006, my Uncle Darryl spoke to me out of his military background. He said that I would not come back to the United States the same man:

such foreign service will forever change me somehow. He was right, of course. I had changed, and yet did not lose my true identity: I was just as much "Justin Lopina" as before. My faith was about the same, my physical appearance was about the same, and my baseline mannerisms were equally familiar. However, my drive to serve and to live for someone else (remember my talk with Heather in chapter 8?) skyrocketed and has never come back down. In fact, it's been in overdrive for so long, my spiritual directors and counselors have had to reign me in and remind me that priesthood is service *and sacrifice*: sometimes, I need to remind myself that my place is first and foremost at the altar. The love of service is a true and worthy gift, but it must eventually lead to the altar. Africa, more than any other factor that I can discern, is the cause for that love of service that has enriched my life beyond measure.

While those things were happening a few thousand miles away, things happened at home during my absence. In 2007, well before my return to the states, my grandmother died and my mother was diagnosed with breast cancer. My grandmother's death came first. I was told that she was running out of time, and I was able to write a farewell letter and get it to the states fast enough for her to receive it in time. I remain thankful to the Lord for that one - overseas mail can very easily be delayed for any number of reasons. As she neared the end, I had trouble concentrating on the news. There was a relatively minor political dispute in Burkina at that time, and while we were not evacuated to another country, we were put on something similar to lockdown. We were instructed to remain in our villages for as long as possible (your village is your safest place during such times), and not to travel to the capital until the all-clear was given. I happened to be visiting friends in a neighboring district, so I was more than a full day's travel away from my village when the news hit. So of all places on earth, I faced the reality of my grandmother's death in the grubby hotel room of an unfamiliar town while eating pickles, cookies, and other canned or ready-to-eat foods with a fellow volunteer who was also unable to travel home. I can still remember that exact evening in precise detail, when I was concentrating most heavily on my grandmother's imminent death. Bryan and I were on our beds, in semi-low lighting in that hotel room that was little more than a cement cube. The walls were a reddish-beige, giving the entire room a slightly rusty color overall. We had both biked from his remote village to his regional capitol, and it was a significantly harder ride than I was accustomed to. So our room largely smelled of sweat, dirt, and pickle brine. Honestly, as awful as that smell might seem, it was entirely familiar to Bryan and me at that point. Besides the fact that I didn't eat pickles all that often, it was essentially the background smell of my entire experience in Burkina Faso. The most unique detail was the fact that I was with Bryan, whom I did not visit very often. So besides a few comments regarding my thoughts, the turmoil of my grandmother's fate was largely internal. On the outside, I mainly recovered with Bryan from our long bike ride, and we concerned ourselves with the political status of the country. The well-being of other volunteers was a difficult consideration to avoid speculating on. In fact, it was hard to concentrate on anything other than the current predicament: we were in more danger than either of us had experienced up to that point, and there was nothing to do but wait and worry. When life returned to normal a few weeks later, I realized that my grandmother deserved better. After all, I was one of only two family members who missed the funeral. Luckily, that fact didn't eat me up: my sister read my letter to everyone at the funeral, and during our final phone call, my grandmother made it perfectly clear that I was not to come home on her account.

Had 2007 ended with no further issues, I probably would have been fine in terms of my overall emotional wellness. However, soon after grandma's passing, I got the news about mom. During our weekly Tuesday phone call, I was informed that my mom certainly had some measure of cancer. Testing was ongoing, but some tough times were ahead for her no matter what. I was furious with myself for being away, and some of that may have been due to my absence during my grandma's death. My mom's diagnosis revealed that the cancer had spread to exactly one lymph node: the minimum amount of cancer you need to have in order to warrant the full treatment of chemotherapy and radiation. After talking to doctors and advisors and friends, she decided to have a full double mastectomy as well as the chemo and radiation. Of all the side effects, my mom was worried the most about losing her hair. My mom, like grandma, forbade me from coming home on her account: after all, my mom's life was not in immediate danger. Even so, I felt terrible for being away.

For my part, I managed two minor acts of familial camaraderie. For starters, if my mother was going to lose her hair, I could follow suit. So one day I went to the village barber and had him shave my head bare - right down to the scalp. It was horribly traumatic that first time: I looked so strange that it felt like that barber shaved my whole face off. I dealt with my new look by wearing a bandana out of doors, which backfired on me: the next day of class, I learned that only women wear bandanas in that country. My students' repeated use of the term "mademoiselle Lopina" was pretty much a dead giveaway. From there, I chose to simply deal with a bald head in public. Amusingly, that little tradition of mine carries on to this day: I shave my head at least once a year, partially to remember what my mom went through and partially to shock me out of my comfort zone a bit. To be fair, however, I no longer go straight to the scalp as it isn't ultimately worth that amount of effort.

The second act I pulled off was my departure date. As an education volunteer teaching in an ordinary secondary school, I was essentially done with my work in early June and due to depart in late August. I was fatigued from life in Africa and I felt the need to be with family

140

more than at the bar drinking beer with the other teachers and middle-class men of Gorgadji. The administration recognized my need to head home and honored my request for an early departure. Although I did not manage to get home until my mother had finished her treatments, I was nevertheless there to be present for her recovery. That part of the process may not be terribly dramatic or extreme, but it is still challenging and demoralizing time.

The story told thus far is the one from my perspective, but an even more powerful story was quietly unfolding in its own right. My mother, by way of her cancer, had undergone a paradigm shift: the way she looked at the world had changed, and it was a lasting change at that. Perhaps somewhat predictably, my mother began with anger toward God and/or the medical world. She asked God the "why me?" question a few hundred times, and largely lost herself in the chaotic process of seeking out a good reason for her disease. She didn't really find one, as would be expected; even people who find a spiritual or ultimate reason for their misfortune would still consider giving up that blessing in exchange for their original way of life, free of misfortune.

Eventually, that first phase of recovery ran its course and life mostly returned to normal. Her hair grew back after about six months, and it took a fraction of that time to grow accustomed to mom with full head of hair (albeit on the short side). Her energy returned, and every follow-up test she had confirmed that she was indeed 100% cancer-free. As typical for cancer survivors, she goes in once a year for a screening, in case the cancer had returned. It's always a stressful time of the year, even though she's been declared cancer-negative every single time.

It is possible, in the strictest sense of the word, that my mother's life could return to exactly the same as it was before the initial diagnosis. A slightly shorter haircut than usual and an extra doctor's appointment would be the only evidence that anything serious had happened in 2007. Of course, that's not the way life works: nothing ever goes back to exactly as it was. My mother had been through a traumatic experience, and in spite of a good resolution, the inherent fear of the whole process left its mark on her. Although life would certainly not remain static, there is never any way to predict how someone will react to fear. Some people utterly break; their confidence or boldness shatters and never returns again. For others, the solution to fear is to reinvent oneself: new clothes, new attitude, new personality. A break from the old and weak pre-trauma persona. For my mom, the result wasn't either of those: for her, the mark of fear was a propellant - it was something that accelerated her forward in life for the better. The trauma began with greater fear but ended in greater compassion. She went out of her way to aid others who were going through a cancer diagnosis. Sometimes, that was a simple series of phone calls or home visits as her schedule allowed. At other times, it came in the form of advice or some kind of one-person support group. Once, she offered aid to someone who didn't have family available to care for her post-surgery needs. So that friend stayed at our house, in order for her to recover in the presence of others with the simple care that she occasionally required.

I know that there are other instances of how my mother has grown spiritually and emotionally after her battle with cancer. The moments detailed above are the ones where I was able to directly observe the change. Other moments in life that indicate my mother's fight with cancer have certainly occurred, but the details aren't fully known to me. Therefore, this book can't do them justice, and that's ok. It's something that doesn't need to be fully documented in order for the point to be made: changes are always happening. Sometimes we seek them out, as a free and informed choice. At other times, they happen to us naturally and cannot be stopped; our free will calculates the equation when we choose how to react to that inevitable change.

Change happens all around us: people and places change, and there is absolutely nothing we can actively do about it. Then again, even if change happens when we are on the other side of the globe, we retain the ability to adapt ourselves to that new reality and learn what we can from the development of others. We always retain the ability to learn from others. Or, in the words of Saint Paul:

Do not be conformed to this world, but continuously be transformed by the renewing of your minds so that you may be able to determine what God's will is - what is proper, pleasing, and perfect.
-Rom 12:2, International Standard Version

In essence, that's the entire point of this entire book. To be transformed by the renewal of your mind: the absolute and ultimate solution to the error of conformity. Conformity is what the world demands of us: and it always lessens us on a fundamental level. The opposite of conformity is not rebelliousness nor reactionism. The opposite of conformity is the renewal of your mind: the willingness to observe all that is happening around you, and to learn from what you see, feel, and experience. At times, that means rejecting the world's expectations or status quo. At other times, that means rejecting your own preconceptions in favor of what the world has to offer. As long as you seek out what is proper, pleasing, and perfect, you will never go far astray.

My mother, in one sense, accomplished that process over the course of a few years: she took her cancer and refused to be mastered by it. The cancer did not own her. She owned the cancer, and her soul is immeasurably more powerful as a result. After her own recovery, she had a great inner need to help those in similar circumstances: that is pleasing and proper to God.

What has changed in the last ten years? What has changed in the last two years? What has changed since yesterday? Who do you want to be tomorrow, or next year, or your next milestone year? These are worthy questions to ask! These are questions we can ask ourselves at any time, and those very questions provide us an opportunity to perpetually renew our minds. Good questions, after all, lead to even bigger good questions. Who am I now? Am I really who I think I am? If others do not see me as I wish to be seen, how can I change so that they see a more genuine "me"?

I sincerely hope you've found something worthy of your thought and reflection in these pages. I have no real knowledge or wisdom to offer, beyond the intersection of the beauty of the world and the wonder of God's grace in my life. I know that everyone has a bad year, as surely as everyone has a bad day. I hope that you can believe that even your steps backward can lead you forward on the journey of life: your hardships as well as your mistakes. For in the end, all it truly requires is the renewal of your mind and the refusal to be enslaved by the expectations of the world. I promise that it can be done, in spite of everything against you, and it is my solemn wish that every period of your life is better than the last.

Thank you for reading.

Wherever you are and whatever you do, may God bless you, now and forever.

Father Justin Jopina

About the Author:

Father Justin is a diocesan priest for the Archdiocese of Milwaukee, WI. Ordained in 2014, he has served as a full-time Associate Pastor up to the present day. Most of his Sunday homilies can be viewed on YouTube; his channel and playlists can be easily found by searching "Father Justin's Homilies". He also periodically celebrates Mass for the Heart of the Nation, intended for broadcast. Masses for Heart of the Nation can also be viewed on YouTube at https://www.youtube.com/user/HeartoftheNation.

Aside from priesthood, Father Justin is a perfectly normal guy. Apart from his periodic habits of jumping out of perfectly good airplanes, expressing himself through the art of dance and fire (at the same time), and steadily amassing a collection of educationally-relevant stuffed animals and hand puppets.

Made in the USA
Middletown, DE
17 February 2018